· PEOPLES OF AFRICA ·

PEOPLES OF WEST AFRICA

THE DIAGRAM GROUP

Facts On File, Inc.

Peoples of Africa: Peoples of West Africa

Diagram Visual Information Ltd

Editorial director:	Bridget Giles
Contributors:	Trevor Day, Theodore Rowland Entwistle, David Lambert, Keith Lye, Oliver Marshall, Christopher Priest
Editors:	Margaret Doyle, Moira Johnston, Ian Wood
Indexer:	David Harding
Art director/designer:	Philip Patenall
Artists:	Chris Allcott, Darren Bennett, Bob Garwood, Elsa Godfrey, Brian Hewson, Kyri Kyriacou, Janos Marffy, Kathy McDougall Patrick Mulrey, Rob Shone, Graham Rosewarne, Peter Ross
Production director:	Richard Hummerstone
Production:	Mark Carry, Lee Lawrence, Ollie Madden, Philip Richardson, Dave Wilson
Research director:	Matt Smout
Researchers:	Pamela Kea, Chris Owens, Catherine Michard, Neil McKenna

With the assistance of:
Dr. Elizabeth Dunstan, International African Institute, School of Oriental and African Studies, University of London
David Hall, African studies bibliographer at the School of Oriental and African Studies, University of London
Horniman Museum, London
Museum of Mankind library, British Museum
Survival International
WWF-UK

Facts On File, Inc.
11 Penn Plaza
New York NY 10001

Library of Congress Cataloging-in-Publication Data

Peoples of West Africa / the Diagram Group.
      p.   cm. – (Peoples of Africa)
  Includes index.
  ISBN 0-8160-3485-0 (alk. paper)
  1. Ethnology–Africa, West. 2. Africa, West–Social life and customs. I. Diagram Group. II. Series: Peoples of Africa (New York, N.Y.)
  GN652.5.P48 1997
  305.800966–dc20   96-38737

Facts On File books are available at special discounts when purchased in bulk quantities for businesses, associations, institutions, or sales promotions. Please call our Special Sales Department in New York at 212/967-8800 or 800/322-8755.

You can find Facts On File on the World Wide Web at http://www.factsonfile.com

Cover design by Molly Heron

Printed in the United States of America

RRD DIAG 10 9 8 7 6 5 4 3

This book is printed on acid-free paper

Contents

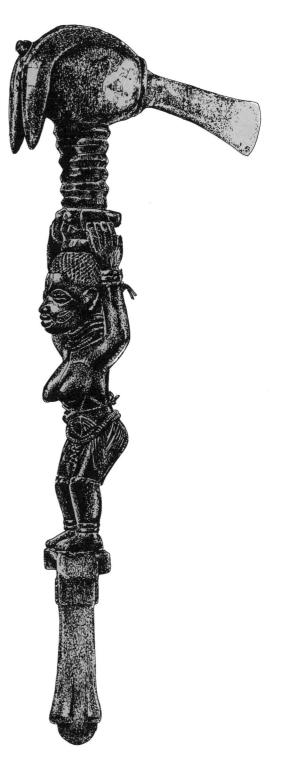

Foreword

Peoples of West Africa, the second volume in the Facts On File *Peoples of Africa* series, focuses on the west of the continent. This area covers the nations of Benin, Burkina Faso, Cameroon, Chad, Gambia, Ghana, Guinea, Guinea-Bissau, Ivory Coast, Liberia, Mali, Mauritania, Niger, Nigeria, Senegal, Sierra Leone, and Togo. The island nation of Cape Verde off the west coast is also part of this region.

Inside this volume the reader will find:

- **The region:** preliminary pages describing the region in depth – its land, climate, vegetation, and wildlife – and others providing a historical overview and a current political profile of the region.

- **The people:** profiles of thirteen major ethnic groups within West Africa, describing the **history, language, ways of life, social structure,** and **culture and religion** of each group. A map has been included for each ethnic group to show the general region a group inhabits or is most concentrated in. The peoples profiles are arranged alphabetically. They are not encyclopedic; instead, they highlight particular aspects of a culture, focusing on fascinating details that will remain with the reader.

- **Special features:** tinted pages interspersed throughout the volume, each on a particular topical or cultural subject. Historical theme spreads, such as that on the Kingdom of Benin, demonstrate the lasting influence of past civilizations. Other features illustrate the great variety to be found in food and drink, music, and hairstyles.

- **Language appendix:** a diagrammatic outline of the African language families and their subfamilies and groups that can be used to locate the languages of the peoples profiled and to see how they relate to other African languages.

- **Glossary and index**: following the profiles and features are a comprehensive glossary defining the unfamiliar terms used and a complete index to the volume. Words that appear in the glossary have been printed in roman in special features and *italics* elsewhere.

Taken as a whole, *Peoples of West Africa* is intended to project a living portrait of the region that, with the other volumes in the series, provides the reader with a memorable snapshot of Africa as a place of rich heritage, far-reaching influence, and ongoing cultural diversity.

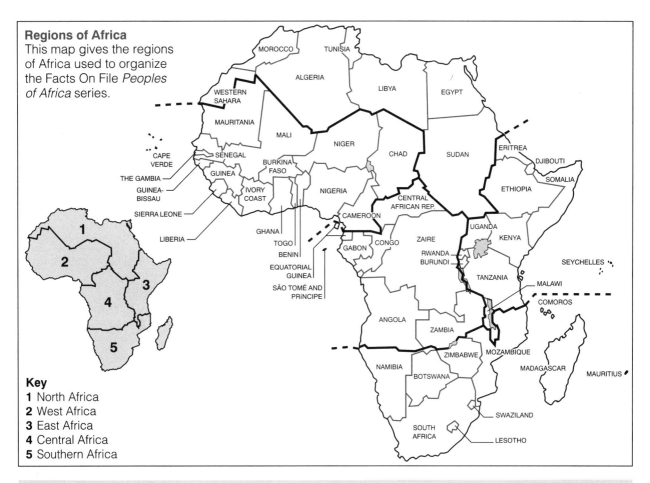

Regions of Africa

This map gives the regions of Africa used to organize the Facts On File *Peoples of Africa* series.

MOROCCO
TUNISIA
ALGERIA
LIBYA
EGYPT
WESTERN SAHARA
MAURITANIA
MALI
NIGER
CHAD
SUDAN
ERITREA
DJIBOUTI
CAPE VERDE
SENEGAL
BURKINA FASO
SOMALIA
THE GAMBIA
GUINEA
ETHIOPIA
GUINEA-BISSAU
IVORY COAST
NIGERIA
CENTRAL AFRICAN REP.
SIERRA LEONE
CAMEROON
UGANDA
GHANA
KENYA
LIBERIA
TOGO
GABON
CONGO
ZAIRE
BENIN
RWANDA
BURUNDI
SEYCHELLES
EQUATORIAL GUINEA
TANZANIA
SÃO TOMÉ AND PRÍNCIPE
MALAWI
COMOROS
ANGOLA
ZAMBIA
MOZAMBIQUE
NAMIBIA
ZIMBABWE
MADAGASCAR
MAURITIUS
BOTSWANA
SWAZILAND
SOUTH AFRICA
LESOTHO

Key
1 North Africa
2 West Africa
3 East Africa
4 Central Africa
5 Southern Africa

A word about ethnic groups

The series *Peoples of Africa* focuses on ethnic groups or peoples, useful but difficult-to-define terms. In the past, the word "tribe" was used to describe ethnic groupings, but this is today considered an offensive and arbitrary label. It is incorrect to refer to a group of people who may number in the hundreds of thousands and who have a long history of nation building as a tribe. "Tribe" is now generally used only to describe a basic political unit that exists within some larger ethnic groups, not to describe the group itself. So what is an ethnic group? An ethnic group is distinct from race or nationality; the former is rarely used today because it requires broad and inaccurate generalizations; and the latter describes only the national boundaries within which a person is born or lives. Both categories are fraught with difficulty. For the purposes of this series, the term "ethnic group" is used to describe people who have a common language, history, religion, and cultural and artistic heritage; they may also have a common way of life and often live within the same geographical area.

There are probably more than a thousand ethnic groups in all of Africa. Many are related to one another, often in complex ways. Groups have subgroups and even sub-subgroups. Intermarriage, colonialism, conquest, and migration through the ages have led to many combinations and to an intermixing of influences. In our series we have chosen to focus on only a fraction of Africa's many ethnic groups. A number of factors – including population figures, available information, and recognition outside Africa – were used in making the selection. To a certain extent, however, it was an arbitrary choice, but one that we hope offers a vibrant picture of the people of this continent.

West Africa today

In under forty years, West Africa has emerged from colonialism into nationhood. The path has not been smooth. Ethnic and religious differences combined with economic problems – including falls in commodity prices for such key exports as cocoa – have caused instability. Most countries have resorted to one-party or military rule to maintain order. By the mid-1990s, however, many West African nations had either returned to democratic rule or were in transition to democracy. Sierra Leone, Gambia, Liberia, and Nigeria are exceptions. While Gambia enjoyed nearly thirty years of democracy until a coup in 1994, Nigeria has had civilian rule for only nine years since 1960. This oil-rich nation is West Africa's giant, containing almost half the region's population. Yet its gross national product (GNP) per capita (for each person) is below the regional average. West African countries with lower per capita GNPs than Nigeria include Sierra Leone and Liberia, which have both suffered civil wars. By contrast, Cameroon and Senegal have enjoyed relative stability; their governments have led the way in successfully exploiting limited resources.

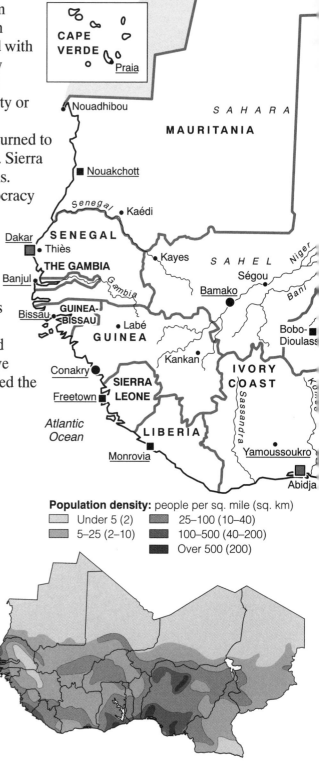

Population density: people per sq. mile (sq. km)

Under 5 (2) 25–100 (10–40)
5–25 (2–10) 100–500 (40–200)
Over 500 (200)

Country	Population (1994: 000s)	Area (sq. mi)	Per capita GNP (1994: US$)
Benin	5,246	43,484	370
Burkina Faso	10,046	105,869	300
Cameroon	12,780	183,569	680
Cape Verde	381	1,557	920
Chad	6,183	495,755	180
The Gambia	1,081	4,361	330
Ghana	16,944	91,985	410
Guinea	6,501	94,926	520
Guinea-Bissau	1,050	13,945	240
Ivory Coast	13,780	124,504	610
Liberia	2,941	42,990	675 (1992)
Mali	10,462	478,821	250
Mauritania	2,217	397,955	480
Niger	8,846	489,191	230
Nigeria	108,467	356,669	280
Senegal	8,300	75,955	600
Sierra Leone	4,402	27,699	160
Togo	4,010	21,925	320

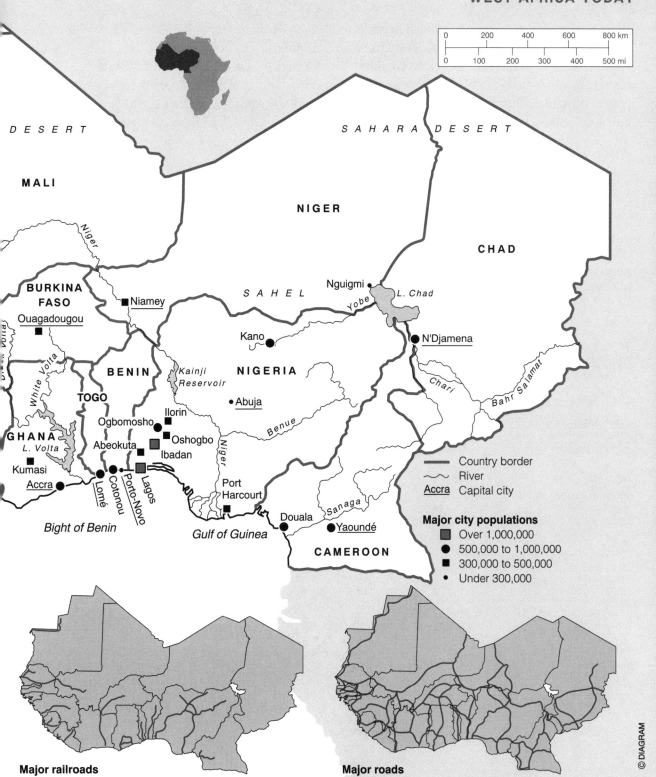

0	200	400	600	800 km
0	100	200	300	400	500 mi

D E S E R T

MALI

S A H A R A   D E S E R T

NIGER

CHAD

Niger

BURKINA FASO

Ouagadougou

■ Niamey

S A H E L

Nguigmi •

L. Chad

Yobe

● N'Djamena

Kano ●

BENIN

Kainji Reservoir

NIGERIA

Chari

Bahr Salamat

TOGO

White Volta

Black Volta

• Abuja

Ogbomosho

Ilorin ■

Benue

GHANA

L. Volta

Abeokuta

■ Oshogbo

Ibadan

Niger

Kumasi ■

Accra ●

Lomé

Cotonou

Porto-Novo

Lagos

Port Harcourt ■

Douala ●

Sanaga

● Yaoundé

Bight of Benin

Gulf of Guinea

CAMEROON

— Country border
〜 River
<u>Accra</u> Capital city

Major city populations
▮ Over 1,000,000
● 500,000 to 1,000,000
■ 300,000 to 500,000
• Under 300,000

Major railroads

Major roads

© DIAGRAM

Land

West Africa is bordered on the north by the Sahara Desert, to the west and south by the Atlantic Ocean, and to the southeast by the highlands of Cameroon. West Africa's rocks range from ancient granites to more recent volcanic outflows. Valuable minerals and fossil fuels form deposits in parts of the region. In a number of countries facing the coast, people mine iron ore, bauxite, tin, antimony, manganese, gold, diamonds, phosphates, coal, and oil. Apart from the mainly narrow, lowland coastal strip, most land consists of plateaus

Flat land above 600 ft (180 m)

Although most of West Africa is flat, the region stands well above sea level. There are three main plateau levels: 600–1,000 ft (180–300 m), 1,500–2,000 ft (450–600 m), and 3,000–4,000 ft (900–1,200 m). Occasional, solitary rocky hills or mountains called *inselbergs* stick up like islands from these plateaus. Some of the higher plateaus end in steep cliffs. The highest plateaus include the Guinea Highlands in the southwest, Nigeria's Jos Plateau, and the Adamawa Highlands, which straddle Nigeria and Cameroon's border. The people who live on these uplands are often descended from war refugees who moved uphill to seek safety or are migrants drawn by the cooler climate.

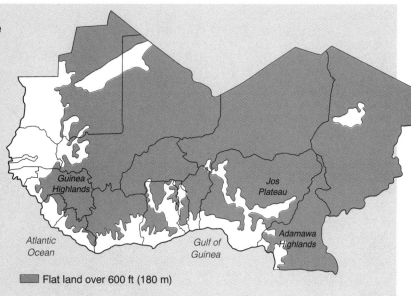

Mountains above 4,500 ft (1,350 m)

West Africa's highest peaks are volcanoes. At 13,451 ft (4,100 m) high, Mount Cameroon – near the coast of Cameroon – is the tallest in West Africa. Cameroon's volcanic soil provides some of the most fertile farmland in West Africa. Molten rock from volcanoes also helped to build the Adamawa Highlands of Cameroon and Nigeria, the Jos Plateau in Nigeria, and Emi Koussi – a peak in northern Chad. At 11,204 ft (3,415 m), Emi Koussi is the highest point in the Tibesti Mountain range. Peaks more than 6,000 ft (1,800 m) high occur in central Niger's Aïr Mountains and in the southwest where the Guinea Highlands cross Sierra Leone.

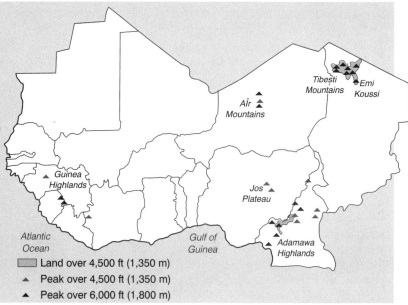

more than 600 ft (180 m) high with some mountains in the north and south. Rivers have cut valleys in the mountains, but most northern rivers flow only briefly when flash floods fill their beds. West Africa occupies nearly one-quarter of the African continent and houses approximately one-third of its total population – the vast majority of whom live in Nigeria. Other densely populated areas include the valleys of the major rivers such as the Senegal, Gambia, and Volta.

Coastal lowlands

The coast of West Africa is low lying. It is backed by a low plain, which occurs before the ground rises inland. West Africa's southern coast is fairly straight, with offshore sandbars that trap long, narrow strips of water which form lagoons. From northern Sierra Leone northward, much of the coast has inlets called *rias* where the sea has drowned river valleys and bitten deeply into the land. Parts of the West African coast are heavily populated as people seeking work have flocked into coastal cities and ports such as Dakar in Senegal and Lagos in Nigeria. Many coastal people fish in the sea from powered canoes, launches, or trawlers.

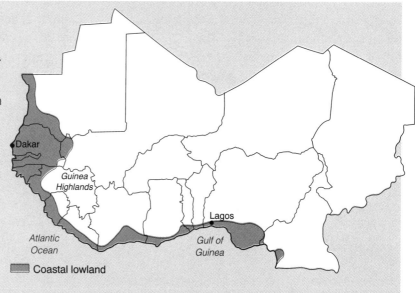

Rivers and lakes

The Niger is West Africa's largest river and the third longest in Africa. In southern Nigeria, it ends in a *delta* (an apron of land built into the sea by mud deposited by the river). One of the world's largest and shallowest natural lakes is Lake Chad, which lies in Chad, Niger, and Nigeria. Its size varies from year to year according to rainfall. West Africa also has one of the world's largest artificial lakes, Lake Volta – formed by Ghana's Akosombo Dam. The rivers and lakes provide freshwater fishing and irrigation for crops. Dammed rivers also supply hydroelectric power. Navigable stretches of the Niger, Senegal, and Gambia rivers allow the transportation of both goods and people.

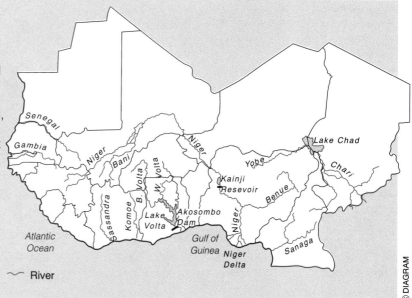

Climate

West Africa has a mostly hot climate and the great majority of the region has both wet and dry seasons. The region is hot as it is almost completely within the tropics: most of West Africa lies between the equator and the Tropic of Cancer. Inland areas are coolest when the Sun moves south – when it is winter in the Northern Hemisphere. The coast is coolest when the Sun moves north – when it is summer in the Northern Hemisphere. Just south of the Sahara Desert, the climate is semiarid with great swings in daily temperature from hot to cold and little rainfall. In fact, much of northern West Africa has hardly any rain all year round. The inland regions south of the semiarid zone have a hot, tropical climate with both wet and dry seasons. Rainfall is heaviest during the wet season. Forested regions on the southern Atlantic coast have tropical wet climates, meaning that they are virtually always hot and wet.

Winds

During the year air masses shift, setting up winds that blow over West Africa from different directions in different seasons. Between November and April, air pressure is higher over the Sahara Desert than over the Atlantic Ocean, which lies to the west and south of West Africa. This pressure difference causes a strong wind to blow from the center of the Sahara over West Africa and toward the Atlantic. This cool, dry, dusty northeast wind is called the *harmattan*. When it blows, dust and sand gets into buildings, clothes, and into people's eyes and mouths. From May through October, air pressure is higher over the sea than over the land. Between these months, moist southwesterly winds blow into West Africa from the Atlantic.

Temperature

West Africa is always warm or hot except on the high mountains and in the Sahara Desert, which experiences great swings of temperature. The desert's greatest extremes are between day and night. At night, temperatures can sink to 4 °C (39 °F) as heat escapes into the cloudless sky. By day, they can soar above 43 °C (109 °F). At its hottest, the western Sahara is almost as hot as Death Valley, California, which often tops 51 °C (124 °F) in summer. At Dakar on the coast of Senegal, the annual average-temperature range is only between 21 and 28 °C (70 and 82 °F). Inland to the north, temperatures fluctuate more according to the season. The temperature range can be as much as 12 to 29 °C (54 to 84 °F).

Rainfall

Annual rainfall ranges from less than 1 in. (2.5 cm) in the southern Sahara, to more than 100 in. (254 cm) on parts of the southern coast, and to nearly 33 ft. (10 m) in the wettest parts of Cameroon. May through October is West Africa's rainiest time, as moist sea winds blow inland from the Atlantic. November through April is drier, as the harmattan wind from the Sahara blows west and south and stops moist sea air reaching the interior. The dry regions stay dry because they lie under a mass of dry, high-pressure air sinking over the Sahara. Wet regions are wet because they lie under a mass of moist rising air largely drawn from the Atlantic. As this air rises it cools, and its moisture condenses into raindrops.

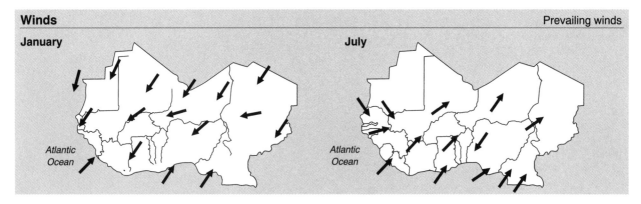

Winds   Prevailing winds

January   July

Atlantic Ocean

Atlantic Ocean

Temperature

Actual surface temperature

January

☐ Below 20 °C (68 °F)   ▨ 20–25 °C (68–77 °F)   ▩ Above 25 °C (77 °F)

July

▨ Below 25 °C (77 °F)   ▨ 25–30 °C (77–86 °F)   ▩ Above 30 °C (86 °F)

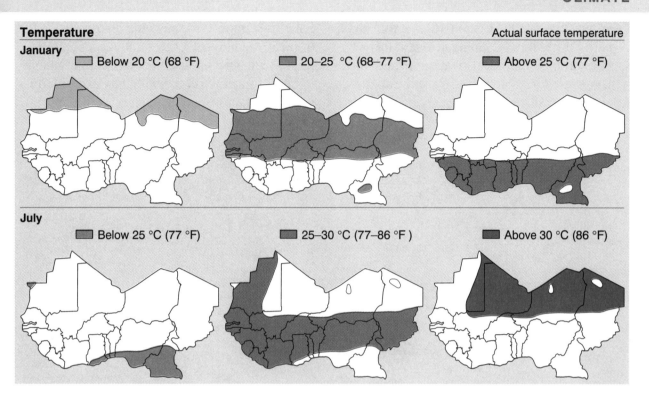

Rainfall

Total rainfall

November to April

☐ Below 10 in. (25 cm)   ▨ 10–30 in. (25–76 cm)   ▩ 30–60 in. (76–152 cm)
▩ Above 60 in. (152 cm)

May to October

☐ Below 10 in. (25 cm)   ▨ 10–30 in. (25–76 cm)   ▩ 30–60 in. (76–152 cm)
▩ Above 60 in. (152 cm)

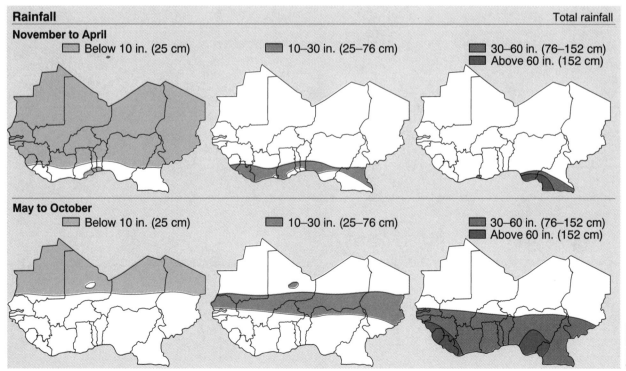

Vegetation

From north to south, West Africa has four main belts of vegetation: the Sahara Desert, the semidesert Sahel, tropical *savanna* (grassland with scattered trees and shrubs), and tropical forests. The Sahara is arid (hot and dry); the Sahel is semiarid; the savanna regions have a tropical wet and dry climate; and the forested regions a tropical wet climate. Rainfall, which increases form north to south, is a particularly important factor. Each zone has a different set

Desert

A deep belt of the Sahara Desert stretches across the almost rainless northern part of West Africa. Only plants adapted to long, hot periods of little rain can survive here. Small shrubs and low, thorny acacia trees put down deep roots to reach underground moisture. Leaves reduced to small spines have small surface areas that limit the amount of water lost through evaporation. Some plants store water and food in underground bulbs. The seeds of short, hard grasses can persist in the soil for years, sprouting quickly after rain to form temporary pastures. Lines of tamarisks (small trees with slender branches), oleanders (evergreen shrubs), euphorbias (cactuslike shrubs and trees), and other small trees and shrubs mark the course of *wadis* (dry river beds). In *oases* (fertile pockets in the desert), date palms and doum palms rise above citrus-fruit trees that shade vegetable plots, while grains such as barley, millet, and wheat thrive in the open.

Typical plants
1 Acacia
2 Short grass
3 Date palm
4 Doum palm

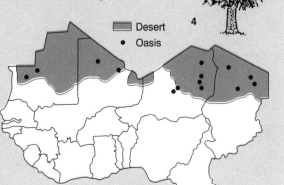

Desert
• Oasis

Semidesert

South of the Sahara lies the Sahel – a largely semidesert area that often suffers from *drought* (inadequate rainfall). Over much of this region, the main vegetation is scattered bunches of grasses. New shoots sprout after the light seasonal rains forming temporary pastures. Drought-resistant shrubby euphorbias thrive in the Sahel. In the north, the driest part, the few trees are mainly acacias. Farther south, where the rainfall is higher and more certain, stands an occasional drought-resistant baobab tree or doum palm. Other tall plants found in this part of West Africa include dracaena (treelike plants that have sword-shaped leaves which form spiky tufts at the tips of branches). Drought-resistant grains such as sorghum are grown in some areas. Since the 1960s, recurring drought and overuse of this fragile land have helped to turn patches of the semidesert into desert. This process – known as *desertification* – involves a loss of vegetation and a decrease in soil fertility.

Typical plants
1 Euphorbia
2 Acacia
3 Doum palm
4 Baobab

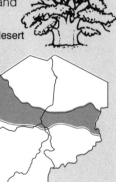

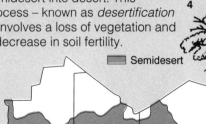

Semidesert

of plants that is adapted to the varying climatic conditions. In addition to these main vegetation zones, a few pockets of *montane forest* (cool and moist forests) – sometimes called "mist forests" – and montane woodlands grow in regions above 3,000 ft (900 m) above sea level. These highlands have temperate species that are not found at lower levels and which are suited to the cooler climate.

Tropical savanna

Tropical savanna is a mixture of grassland with scattered trees and shrubs. In West Africa, tropical savanna forms a broad belt between the Sahel to the north and the tropical forests to the south. The drier, northern savanna is open, parklike countryside with thorny acacia and thick-trunked baobab trees. These trees shed their leaves to survive the long, seasonal droughts. The grasses grow in tussocks and are taller than those of the Sahel. Shorter grasses grow on dry stony land. The moist, southern savanna is a mixture of woods and grasslands. Dense woods line some rivers. Grasses such as elephant grass grow more than head high and tall evergreen trees rim the rivers. Tall, reedlike papyrus plants can be found in the rivers. Away from the rivers, trees tend to shed their leaves to survive the seasonal droughts. Food crops such as corn, millet, rice, and sorghum and cash crops such as cotton, coffee, and *groundnuts* (peanuts) are grown in the savanna regions.

Typical plants
1 Elephant grass
2 Gum arabic acacia
3 Baobab
4 Papyrus

Tropical savanna

Tropical forest

Tropical forests occur in moist, lowland West Africa south of the savannas. Low, muddy coasts and river mouths are rimmed by *mangrove forests* – also called *mangrove swamps* – upto several miles wide. Mangrove trees have networks of long, stiltlike, speading roots that anchor them in the water. These forests are important as they provide breeding places for fish and help build up dry land by holding silt. Many have been cleared for rice cultivation though. Away from the coast stand dense, tropical *rainforests*. Hundreds of different species of trees exist in rainforests. Although the majority are broadleaved evergreens, palms and tree ferns can also be found. Tall trees called *emergents* soar above others that form the upper *canopy*. Climbing plants, *epiphytes* (plants that grow on other plants but are not parasites), and other small plants grow on the branches. Few plants grow in the dim light on the forest floor. Rainforests are being cut down, however, to provide timber or to clear land to grow crops on.

Tropical forest plants
1 Mangrove
2 Ebony
3 Oil palm

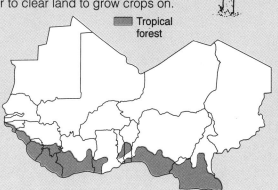

Tropical forest

Wildlife

West Africa belongs to the *Ethiopian faunal realm* – a biogeographical zone which includes most of sub-Saharan Africa. Mammals of this realm include lions, antelopes, giraffes, and elephants, most of which have been displaced by farming as it encroaches on their territory, and hunting, which has already decimated many wildlife populations. Elephant herds once roamed the grasslands but are now virtually extinct in West Africa. Each vegetation zone in West Africa – the Sahara Desert, the semidesert Sahel, tropical *savannas* (grasslands with

Desert

Creatures that live in the desert are suited to the hot, dry environment. The fennec (desert fox) and the desert hedgehog both have large ears that radiate heat, helping to keep them cool. Small rodents called jerboas bound over open spaces on long hind legs. Smaller creatures tend to hide from the Sun's heat by day and come out to feed at night. Larger mammals such as the addax (a large antelope with twisted horns) and dama gazelle (a small, slender antelope) have been hunted almost to extinction. Birds range from the houbara bustard (a large bird as tall as a turkey) to smaller species such as larks and pigeonlike sandgrouse. Birds of prey also live in the desert, certain types of falcon for example. Skinks (shiny lizards) number among the reptiles. *Invertebrates* (animals without backbones) include ant lions (meat-eating insects) and desert locusts.

Typical animals
1 Addax
2 Dama gazelle
3 Fennec
4 Jerboa
5 Lanner falcon
6 Bifasciated lark
7 Pintail sandgrouse
8 Sand skink
9 Desert locust

Semidesert

In the Sahel – the semidesert region south of the Sahara – creatures have to be able to cope with dry conditions. Consequently, some desert species occur in the Sahel. Semidesert plant-eating animals include two kinds of antelope: the scimitar oryx (a large antelope with straight horns) and the dorcas gazelle (a small, slender antelope). Other antelopes may briefly move in from the grasslands. The antelopes attract visits from large predators such as cheetahs. Cheetahs normally live on the grassy plains of the savanna regions. Smaller game provides food for the caracal (a wildcat) and various jackals (wild dogs). Jackals also feed off dead animals that they find. Birds of prey such as kites feed of small mammals, insects, and reptiles. Vipers and other snakes can also be found in the Sahel. Invertebrates include termites, beetles, and desert locusts.

Typical animals
1 Scimitar oryx
2 Dorcas gazelle
3 Cheetah
4 Caracal
5 Golden jackal
6 Swallow-tailed kite
7 Saw-scaled viper
8 Desert locust

scattered trees and shrubs), and tropical forests – has its own set of wild animals. Many of these live in more than one zone however. Topi antelopes (antelopes with curved, angular horns) can be found in both semidesert and savanna regions. Different varieties of leopards live either in the savanna or the forest. Snakes such as the African python can live in both savannas and forests. Also, the ecologically rich *rainforests* of West Africa probably house many species not yet identified.

Tropical savanna

West Africa's tropical grasslands have many large, plant-eating mammals. Giraffes browse on treetops; roan antelopes (reddish-brown antelopes) graze in moist, open woodlands; topi antelopes eat the dry grass that others ignore; warthogs eat short grass and roots; African buffaloes – relatives of the North American bison – munch grass, shoots, leaves, and twigs. Baboons (large, fierce monkeys with short tails) also live in the savannas, feeding on the ground and sleeping in trees or caves. The chief enemies of warthogs and antelopes are the predatory lions, leopards, and cheetahs. Hunting and the extension of farming in the savanna regions has lead to a decrease in the numbers of larger animals though. Eagles, hawks, hornbills, African pythons, and other birds and snakes prey on small mammals and birds.

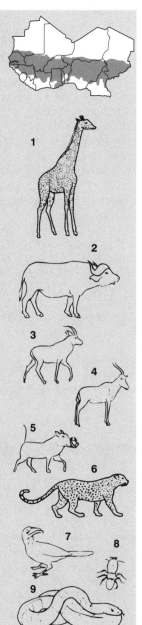

Typical animals
1 Giraffe
2 African buffalo
3 Roan antelope
4 Topi antelope
5 Warthog
6 Leopard
7 Abyssinian ground hornbill
8 Termite
9 African python

Tropical forest

The mangrove forests on the coast are home to sea cows (sea-dwelling mammals) called manatees and a great variety of marine life. A huge number of species live in the rainforests. Climbing animals such as monkeys and gibbons live in the upper branches – including the rare Diana monkey. Forest elephants also live in the rainforests. Duikers (short, compact antelopes) roam the poorly-lit forest floor. Its soil and leaf litter hide scorpions and insects, which are prey to reptiles, predatory birds such as shrikes, and mammals including the strange, scaly pangolin, which eats ants. Small mammals are prey to the African python, which can climb trees. Rivers and swamps contain African clawless otters and the rare pygmy hippopotamus. Once-common creatures are becoming scarce as the rainforests are cut down.

Typical animals
1 Manatee
2 Diana monkey
3 Western baboon
4 Pangolin
5 Banded duiker
6 African clawless otter
7 Pygmy hippopotamus
8 Bare-headed rock fowl
9 Scorpion

Chronology

The artistic achievements of the Nok Culture (c. 500 BCE – 200 CE) include superb terra-cotta sulptures such as this head.

In the ninth century, the Igbo Ukwu Culture of Nigeria produces fine bronze artifacts, such as this bowl and stand.

During the period 1500 to 1800 – the "Era of Firearms and the Slave Trade" in West Africa – the Portuguese introduce firearms to the coastal states of West Africa. This Benin "bronze" depicts a Portuguese soldier with his gun.

WEST AFRICAN EVENTS	WORLD EVENTS
Countries or locations in parentheses give the modern-day locations of the states. Dates of independence appear in a table after the chronology.	
to 1000 CE	
500 BCE Nok Culture in existence (Nigeria)	**510 BCE** Republic of Rome established
c. 1 CE Start of dispersal of Bantu peoples	**30 CE** Jesus of Nazareth crucified
200 Nok Culture ends	
300 Empire of Ghana emerges (Mali)	**455** Vandals sack Rome
c. 700s Igbo Ukwu Culture in existence (Nigeria)	**622** Muhammad's flight to Medina: founding of Islam
c. 750 Kingdom of Kangaba, from which the Empire of Mali emerges, is founded (Mali). Songhay state emerges (Mali)	**624** T'ang dynasty unites China
c. 800 Kingdom of Kanem emerges (Lake Chad region)	**793** Viking raids begin in Europe
800s Takrur founded (Senegal)	
1001–1500	
1050 Islam introduced to West Africa	**1066** Normans conquer England
c. 1150 Empire of Ghana at its height	
1200s Kingdom of Benin emerges (Nigeria). Mossi states begin to be established (Ghana)	**c. 1150** Angkor Wat built in Cambodia
1230 Kanem at its height	**c. 1200** Inca dynasty founded by Manco Capac
1235 Empire of Mali founded (Mali)	
c. 1240 Mali absorbs Ghana and Songhay	**1206** Genghis Khan begins Mongol conquest of Asia
c. 1250 Takrur absorbed by Mali	
1300 Yoruba state of Oyo is established (Nigeria)	**1215** Magna Carta signed in England
c. 1325 Empire of Mali at its height	
1340s Songhay independent from Mali	**1346–9** "Black Death" ravages much of Europe
c. 1350 Hausa city-states emerge (Nigeria)	
1386 State of Borno established (Lake Chad region)	**1368** Ming dynasty begins in China
1400s Wolof Empire founded (Senegal)	**1492** Christopher Columbus discovers New World
1443 Portuguese establish first fort on coast (Mauritania)	
c. 1490 Mali eclipsed by Songhay Empire	
1501–1700	
1510 Start of Atlantic slave trade	**1519–22** Magellan's circumnavigation of the world. Hernan Cortés conquers the Aztecs
c. 1515 Songhay at its height	
1526 Borno controls Kanem	
c. 1550 Wolof Empire dissolved. Mali ceases to exsist	**1526** Mughal Empire founded in India
1587 Portuguese take control of Cape Verde Islands	**c. 1550** Potato introduced to Europe from America
1590 Songhay defeated by Moroccans	
1591 Kanem-Borno at greatest extent	
1625 Dahomey (Benin) established	**1619** First African slaves arrive in
1631 England establishes first post on Gold Coast (coastal Ghana)	

WEST AFRICAN EVENTS	WORLD EVENTS
c. 1640 Fante states emerge (Ghana)	Jamestown, Virginia
c. 1650 Sultanate of Wadai founded (Chad)	**1620** *Mayflower*
1670s Asante clans unify (Ghana)	reaches America

1701–1850

1700 Kingdom of Kong emerges (Ivory Coast)	**1776–83** American War of
1727 Dahomey at greatest extent	Independence
1740 State of Segu (Mali) founded	**1789–99** French
1748 Dahomey conquered by Oyo	Revolution
1789 Oyo at greatest extent	**1807** Britain outlaws
1809 Hausa states defeated by Fulani *jihad* (holy war). Sokoto Caliphate founded by Fulani (Nigeria)	slave trade **1816–28** Chile, Argentina, Brazil,
1816 Fante defeated by Asante	Uruguay, and Peru
1818 Dahomey breaks away from Oyo	gain independence
1824– Four major Anglo-Asante wars **1874** leave Asante Empire in disarray	**1845–51** "Potato Famine" in Ireland
1830 Sokoto reaches greatest extent	**1846–8** US at war
1836 Oyo dissolves. Ibadan Empire emerges	with Mexico **1848** Marx and
1847 Liberia established by freed American slaves	Engels publish *Communist*
1850s Wadai at greatest extent	*Manifesto*

1851–1900

1852 Tukolor Empire established (Mali)	**1857–9** Indian
1870s– Second Mandinka Empire **1880s** established (Senegal) as successor to Empire of Mali	Mutiny: India made a British vice-royalty **1861–5** US Civil War
1879 Rabih b. Fadl Allah begins to build empire (Chad/Nigeria)	**1865** US abolishes slavery
c. 1880 European imperialist "Scramble for Africa" begins	**1868** Meiji Restoration in Japan
1892 Dahomey conquered by French	**1869** Suez Canal
1893 Kanem-Borno defeated by Rabih. French defeat Tukolor Empire	opened **1871** German
1895 France forms federation of colonies that becomes French West Africa. Kong Kingdom defeated by Mandinkas	Empire proclaimed **1875** Alexander Graham Bell invents the telephone
1896 Asante made a British colony	**1898** Spanish–
1897 Benin Kingdom and Ibadan Empire conquered by British	American War **1900** Antiforeigner
1898 Second Mandinka Empire conquered by the French	Boxer Rebellion in China

1901–1949

1901 French defeat Empire of Rabih and Mossi states	**1904** Japan and Russia at war
1902 Asante annexed to Gold Coast	**1905** First Russian
1903 Sokoto conquered by British.	Revolution

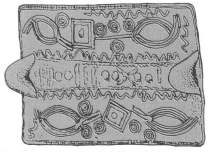

The Asante Empire (1670s–1896) produces many of these gold-weights, actually brass weights that were used to weigh gold dust.

The Kingdom of Benin flourishes in what is now Nigeria from around the 1200s to 1897. This eighteenth-century Benin "bronze" (actually brass) is of a python's head.

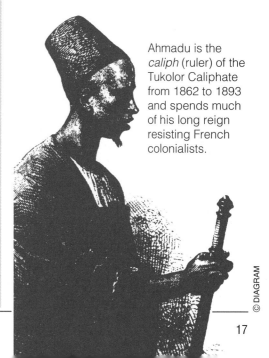

Ahmadu is the *caliph* (ruler) of the Tukolor Caliphate from 1862 to 1893 and spends much of his long reign resisting French colonialists.

© DIAGRAM

Captured Africans after a battle against the French army during the European colonial "Scramble for Africa," which escalates after the 1884 Berlin Conference.

The Organization of African Unity (OAU) is founded in 1963. This stamp marks the OAU summit conference held in Ghana in 1965.

SUMMIT CONFERENCE
ACCRA 1965
OAU
1P
GHANA

In Nigeria, a brutal civil war begins in 1967 when the southeastern region, calling itself Biafra, declares independence.

WEST AFRICAN EVENTS		WORLD EVENTS
1903	Mauritania becomes a French *protectorate* (colony)	1914–18 World War I (WWI)
1909	Wadai defeated by French	1917 US enters
1914	All West Africa, except Liberia, under European domination	WWI. Second Russian Revolution;
1914–1918	West African troops fight on both sides in World War I. Germany defeated in Togoland & Kameruns military campaigns	socialism adopted 1930s Worldwide depression
1916	German colonies of Togoland & Kameruns occupied by Britain and France	1939–45 World War II (WWII) 1946–7 Cold War begins
1939–1945	West African troops fight on Allied side in World War II	1949 Communists control China
1951–1970		
1957	Gold Coast renamed Ghana	1957 North and
1960	Soudan renamed Mali	South Vietnam
1963	Military coups in Dahomey and Togo. Organization of African Unity founded (OAU)	at war 1959 Cuban revolution led by
1966	Popular uprising in Upper Volta topples president; military rule is installed. Military coups in Ghana and Nigeria. Antigovernment guerrilla activity begins in Chad	Fidel Castro 1961 Berlin wall goes up 1962 Cuban missile crisis
1967	Military coups in Dahomey, Sierra Leone, and Togo. Twelve-state structure introduced in Nigeria; Biafran (Nigerian Civil) War begins	1963 US president J.F. Kennedy is assassinated 1968 Martin Luther
1968	End of military rule in Dahomey. Military coup in Mali	King assassinated 1965–73 US
1969	Return to civilian rule in Ghana and Sierra Leone. Military coup in Benin	involvement in Vietnam War 1969 Neil Armstrong
1970	Biafran secessionists defeated. Civilian rule returns in Upper Volta	is first man on the Moon
1971–1980		
1972	Military coups in both Dahomey and Ghana	1973 Oil Crisis and world recession
1974	Military coups in Niger and Upper Volta. Dahomey adopts Marxism-Leninism. Oil boom in Nigeria	after Arabs ban oil sales to the US 1974 Watergate
1975	Dahomey renamed Benin. Mauritania at war with Western Saharan guerrillas. Military coups in Chad and Nigeria	scandal in US. Portuguese Revolution 1975 Communists
1976	Launch of Economic Community of West African States (ECOWAS). Military coup in Togo	reunite Vietnam 1975–9 Khmer Rouge reign of

WEST AFRICAN EVENTS

1977	Nigeria hosts international Black Festival of Arts
1978	End of military rule in Upper Volta. Military coup in Mauritania
1979	Return to civilian rule in Benin and Nigeria. Military coup in Ghana forces elections. Civil war breaks out in Chad. End of Mauritanian-Western Saharan conflict as Mauritania withdraws
1980	Uranium boom in Niger. Military coups in Liberia, Upper Volta, and Guinea-Bissau. Libyan troops invade Chad

1981–1990

1981	Military coup in Ghana
1982	Oil production begins in Benin. Military coup in Upper Volta. Senegal and Gambia unite to form Senegambia Confederation
1983	Military coups in Upper Volta and Nigeria
1984	Military coups in Guinea and Mauritania. Upper Volta renamed Burkina Faso
1985	Military coup in Nigeria. Elections end military rule in Liberia
1986	Volcanic eruption in Cameroon. Nigerian writer Wole Soyinka wins Nobel Prize for Literature
1987	Military coup in Burkina Faso
1989	Senegambia dissolved. Civil war erupts in Liberia. Benin abandons Marxism-Leninism
1990	Government overthrown by rebels in Chad. Popular pressure leads to first multiparty elections in Ivory Coast. President Samuel Doe of Liberia assassinated; civil war escalates. End of one-party politics in Cameroon. Taureg uprising in Niger begins

1991–1996

1991	First free elections in Benin. End of military rule in Burkina Faso. Military coup in Mali. Legalization of opposition parties follows widespread popular unrest in Togo. Multiparty elections end

WORLD EVENTS

terror in Cambodia, ended by Vietnamese invasion
1978–9 Iranian Revolution
1977 Concorde's first flight
1979 Civil wars in Nicaragua and El Salvador
1979–89 USSR invades Afghanistan
1980–8 Iran-Iraq War; US backs Iraq

1982 Falklands War between UK and Argentina
1982–5 Israeli invasion of Lebanon
1985 US unvades Granada
1986 Chernobyl nuclear accident in USSR. "Iran-Contra" scandal in US
1989 Revolutions in Romania, Bulgaria, Czechoslovakia, and East Germany; Berlin Wall demolished. Massacre in Tiananmen Square, Beijing, China
1990 Gulf War begins after Iraq invades Kuwait. East and West Germany reunited. Nelson Mandela released from prison

1991 Break-up of USSR. End of apartheid in South Africa. End of Gulf War. Break-up of Yugoslavia; war

The civil war in Chad begins in 1979. These casualties are awaiting evacuation.

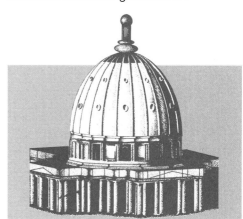

Ex-president of the Ivory Coast, Félix Houphouët-Boigny, commisions the building of the Basilica of Our Lady of Peace, which is built between 1987 and 1989 and is the largest church in the world.

Master Sergeant Samuel Doe takes power after a military coup in Liberia in 1980. His assassination in 1990 leads to the escalation of Liberia's civil war.

© DIAGRAM

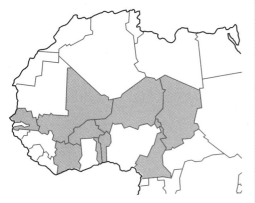

Nigerian officers at the staff college in Jaji. Officers from this college are often involved in the many coups that Nigeria has had since independence in 1960.

After months of pressure from the International Monetary Fund (IMF) and France, these nine West African countries are forced to devalue their currency – the *CFA franc* – by fifty percent. This causes great economic hardship and widespread civil unrest in the *African Franc Zone*.

The writer Ken Saro-Wiwa is one of nine Ogoni activists executed by the Nigerian government in 1995. These executions lead to the suspension of Nigeria's membership of the Commonwealth.

	WEST AFRICAN EVENTS	WORLD EVENTS
	one-party rule in Cape Verde. Rebels launch antigovernment offensive in Sierra Leone sparking a bloody civil war	erupts in Croatia and Slovenia. Civil war breaks out in Somalia
1992	Multiparty politics introduced in Guinea. Elections end military rule in Mali, Mauritania, and Ghana. Military coup in Sierra Leone.	Cold War ends. Riots in LA. War in former Yugoslavia spreads to Bosnia
1993	Elections end military rule in Niger. Military coup in Nigeria annulls recent elections.	Israeli-PLO peace agreement
1994	*African Franc Zone* currency (*CFA*) devalued by fifty percent; Franc Zone countries experience economic hardship; strikes and protests are widespread. Military coup in Gambia. First multiparty elections in Guinea-Bissau. Tuareg sign peace accord with Niger government. Elections in Togo won by opposistion	First nonracial elections in South Africa won by ANC led by Nelson Mandela. Civil war in Rwanda. Peace in Somalia. US intervention in Haiti. Cease-fire announced by IRA
1995	Military government in Nigeria executes nine Ogoni dissidents to international condemnation; Nigeria's membership of the Commonwealth is suspended. Prodemocracy rebels clash with government troops in Chad. Rebel groups in Liberia sign peace agreement. Ethnic fighting in north Ghana. Taureg uprising ended in Mali by peace initiative	Peace agreement in former Yugoslavia. France carries out nuclear tests in Pacific. Israeli prime minister assassinated. Bomb explosion in Oklahoma city, OK, kills 169 people
1996	Military coup in Nigeria. Renewed fighting in Liberia; refugee crisis follows as thousands attempt to flee country in passing ships. Cape Verde and Guniea-Bissau join the Community of Portuguese-Speaking Countries. Rebels and government agree cease-fire in Sierra Leone. Nigeria becomes first African country to win Olympic soccer gold medal	IRA ends cease-fire. TWA airliner explodes off Long Island, NY, killing 230 passengers and crew. Over 600 die in ferry disaster in Lake Victoria. Military coup and ethnic violence in Burundi

COLONIAL OCCUPATION AND INDEPENDENCE

Country	Independence	Occupied*	Colonial powers
Benin (as Dahomey)	Aug 1, 1960	1892	France
Burkina Faso (as Upper Volta)	Aug 5, 1960	1892	France
Cameroon (as German Kameruns, French Cameroons, and British Cameroons)	Jan 1, 1960	1884	Germany 1884–1919; France and Britain divided and took control of Cameroon after Germany's defeat in WWI
Cape Verde	July 5, 1975	1587	Portugal
Chad (as part of French Equatorial Africa)	Aug 11, 1960	1900	France
Ivory Coast (as part of French West Africa)	Aug 7, 1960	1914	France
The Gambia	Feb 18, 1965	1816	Britain
Ghana (as Gold Coast)	March 6, 1957	1896	Britain
Guinea (as French Guinea)	Oct 2, 1958	1898	France
Guinea-Bissau (as Portuguese Guinea)	Sept 10, 1974	1880	Portugal
Liberia			Liberia has been independent since its establishment in 1847
Mali (as Soudan)	June 20, 1960	1898	France
Mauritania (as part of French West Africa)	Nov 28, 1960	1903	France
Niger (as part of French West Africa)	Aug 3, 1960	1908	France
Nigeria	Oct 1, 1960	1880	Britain
Senegal (as part of French West Africa)	June 20, 1960	1890	France
Sierra Leone	April 27, 1961	1787	Britain
Togo (as Togoland)	April 27, 1960	1884	Germany 1884–1919; France 1919–1960

*The years given for the begining of colonial occupation of the modern-day nation states are those by which a significant area of coastal and hinterland territory had been effectively occupied by a colonial power.

This carved stone stands over 6 ft (180 cm) tall and probably dates from the sixteenth century. It comes from the easternmost part of southern Nigeria and appears to represent a village chief. Many civilizations rise and flourish in Africa long before the colonial era, which begins in the late nineteenth century.

© DIAGRAM

Pictorial history

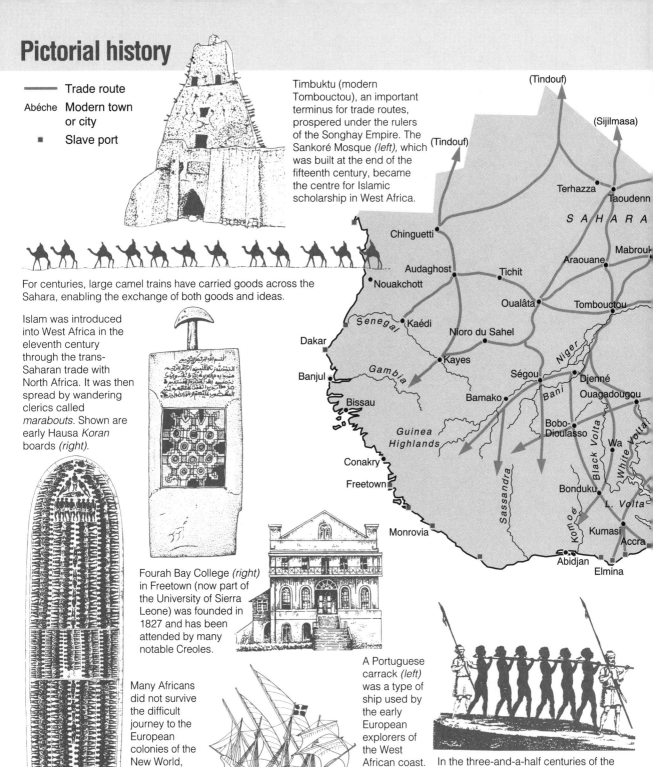

- ——— Trade route
- Abéche Modern town or city
- ■ Slave port

Timbuktu (modern Tombouctou), an important terminus for trade routes, prospered under the rulers of the Songhay Empire. The Sankoré Mosque (left), which was built at the end of the fifteenth century, became the centre for Islamic scholarship in West Africa.

For centuries, large camel trains have carried goods across the Sahara, enabling the exchange of both goods and ideas.

Islam was introduced into West Africa in the eleventh century through the trans-Saharan trade with North Africa. It was then spread by wandering clerics called marabouts. Shown are early Hausa Koran boards (right).

Fourah Bay College (right) in Freetown (now part of the University of Sierra Leone) was founded in 1827 and has been attended by many notable Creoles.

Many Africans did not survive the difficult journey to the European colonies of the New World, but died in the cramped conditions of the slave boats (left).

A Portuguese carrack (left) was a type of ship used by the early European explorers of the West African coast. They found many rich and powerful kingdoms to trade with.

In the three-and-a-half centuries of the Atlantic slave trade over ten million West Africans were enslaved. The survivors of the Atlantic crossing took many aspects of their culture with them that are still very evident in the Americas today.

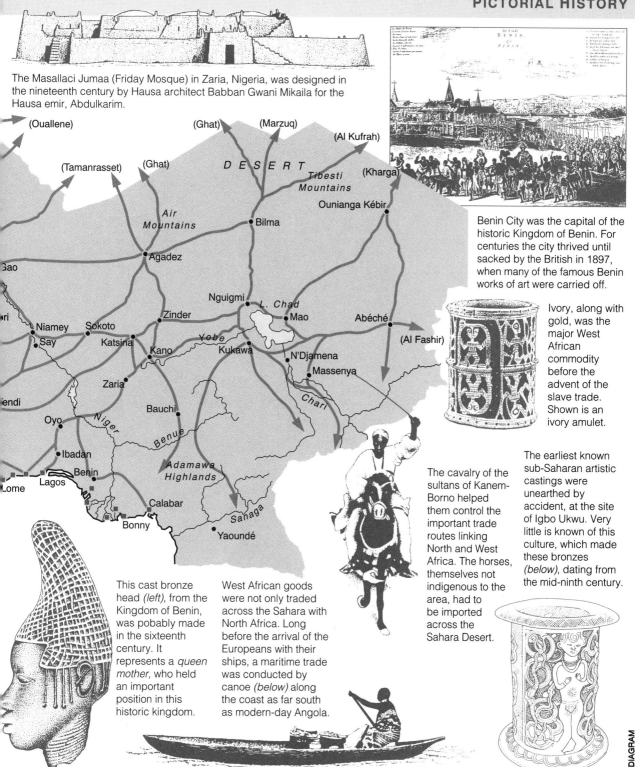

The Masallaci Jumaa (Friday Mosque) in Zaria, Nigeria, was designed in the nineteenth century by Hausa architect Babban Gwani Mikaila for the Hausa emir, Abdulkarim.

Benin City was the capital of the historic Kingdom of Benin. For centuries the city thrived until sacked by the British in 1897, when many of the famous Benin works of art were carried off.

Ivory, along with gold, was the major West African commodity before the advent of the slave trade. Shown is an ivory amulet.

The earliest known sub-Saharan artistic castings were unearthed by accident, at the site of Igbo Ukwu. Very little is known of this culture, which made these bronzes (below), dating from the mid-ninth century.

The cavalry of the sultans of Kanem-Borno helped them control the important trade routes linking North and West Africa. The horses, themselves not indigenous to the area, had to be imported across the Sahara Desert.

This cast bronze head (left), from the Kingdom of Benin, was pobably made in the sixteenth century. It represents a queen mother, who held an important position in this historic kingdom.

West African goods were not only traded across the Sahara with North Africa. Long before the arrival of the Europeans with their ships, a maritime trade was conducted by canoe (below) along the coast as far south as modern-day Angola.

© DIAGRAM

23

Distribution of peoples

1 Moors

The Moors are the largest ethnic group in Mauritania. They are of mixed Berber, Arab, and Black African descent. Most Moors speak Arabic, though a minority speak Berber languages. Historically, the Moors were a nomadic people. In recent years, however, many have become settled. The vast majority of Moors are Muslims and follow the Islamic religion.

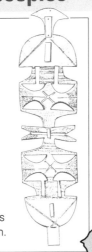

2 Bambara and Malinke

The Bambara and Malinke are both Manding (or Mandinka or Mandingo) peoples. They speak different dialects of the Manding language. Manding peoples are widely spread throughout Mali and neighboring countries. The majority are Muslims. The medieval Empire of Mali was founded by the Malinke people.

3 Mende

The Mende live mostly in Sierra Leone and are the largest single ethnic group in that country. They speak a language also called Mende. Mende society is distinctive for the importance given to various *hale* (secret societies). Until quite recently, knowledge of the workings and functions of these *hale* was kept secret from outsiders.

4 Dogon

The Dogon live in central Mali. The Dogon language is also called Dogon. The Dogon have become famous for their knowledge of astronomy, in particular, of the "Dog Stars," Sirius A and Sirius B. Throughout their history, the Dogon have actively resisted the adoption of Islam or Christianity and most still practice the Dogon religion.

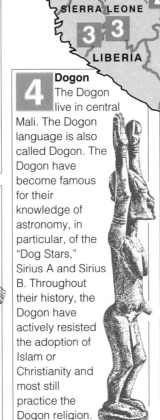

5 Fulani

The Fulani (or Fulbe or Peul) are one of the most widespread ethnic groups of West Africa: Fulani people can be found in most West African countries. The Fulani speak a language called Fulfulde. Some of the Fulani are nomadic whilst others live in settled communities. The Fulani are Muslims and were important in the spread of Islam throughout West Africa. They launched many *jihads* (Islamic holy wars) from the 1700s to 1800s to convert non-Muslims to Islam.

6 Mossi

The Mossi live mostly in Burkina Faso and they speak a language called Moré. The majority of Mossi people follow the Mossi religion. The Mossi are well known for their beautiful masks, which are used in celebrations and at festivals.

MAURITANIA

MALI

Senegal

Niger

SENEGAL

THE GAMBIA

GUINEA-BISSAU

GUINEA

SIERRA LEONE

LIBERIA

IVORY COAST

GHANA

BURKINA FASO

BENIN

TOGO

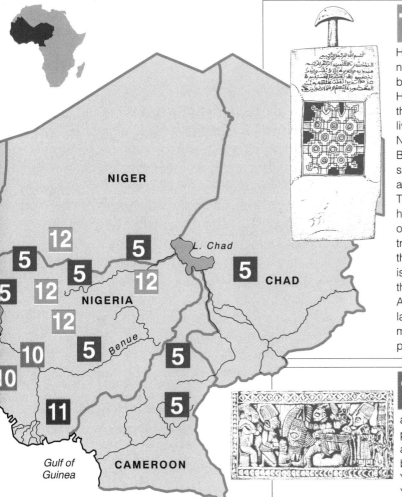

12 Hausa
Although the majority of Hausa people live in northern Nigeria, the base of the historic Hausa city-states, there are others living in southern Niger and northern Benin. The Hausa speak a language also called Hausa. The Hausa people have a long history of involvement in trade. Consequently, the Hausa language is used widely throughout West Africa as a trading language. The vast majority of Hausa people are Muslim.

11 Igbo
The Igbo live mostly in southeastern Nigeria. The five main Igbo groups all speak dialects of the Kwa language. Igbo society is characterized by the avoidance of centralized political systems and, instead, status is accorded by individual merit and achievement. Since the nineteenth century, many Igbo have converted to Christianity. The Igbo religion, however, is still widely practiced.

10 Yoruba
The Yoruba live mostly in southwestern Nigeria and they speak a language also called Yoruba. The Yoruba people have a long history of urbanization and had many town kingdoms, dating from before colonial times. Although many Yorubas are either Muslim or Christian, the Yoruba religion is still flourishing.

7 Asante
The Asante (or Ashanti) live in south-central Ghana. They are the largest ethnic group in Ghana and once formed their own Empire – the Asante Empire, the base of which (the Asante Kingdom) is now part of modern Ghana. The Asante speak a dialect of Twi called Asante. Most are either Christian or Muslim.

8 Ewe
The Ewe live in lands that sit astride the southern half of the border between Ghana and Togo. They speak various dialects of the Ewe language. The Ewe are famous for their strip-weaving skills and produce cloth for many people in West Africa. Although many Ewe people are Christian, the Ewe religion is still widely practiced.

9 Fon
The Fon live mostly in south-central Benin. The speak a language called Twi. From the seventeenth century to the end of the nineteenth century, the Fon Kingdom of Dahomey flourished. The Fon religion involves the worship of gods called *vodu* – of which "voodoo" is a Western corruption.

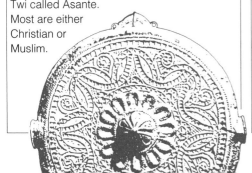

© DIAGRAM

25

Introduction

The peoples of West Africa reflect a wide variety of lifestyles and cultures. This book describes a selected sample of these cultures, where possible detailing contemporary changes and the effects they have had on people's lives.

Historical overview

The Nok Culture (c. 500 BCE to c. 200 CE) of Nigeria is the earliest known civilization in West Africa. By the first millennium, states had arisen all over West Africa. Before the fifteenth century, four great nations dominated the grasslands: the Empire of Ghana, the Empire of Mali, Songhay, and Kanem-Borno. These empires based their prosperity on trading in gold and salt. Meanwhile, in the forest regions on the south coast, kingdoms – such as those of the Yoruba and the Kingdom of Benin – had arisen. Although the Sahara Desert separates West from North Africa, it never formed an uncrossable barrier. For more than 2,000 years, people have made the 1,500-mile (2,400-km) journey – mostly to trade, but both ideas and goods have been exchanged. West Africa's reserves of gold became the major source of supply to the Arab world and, from there, to Europe and Asia.

During the sixteenth century, trade with Europeans grew along the West African coast. The main "commodities" were gold and slaves, the Europeans needed slaves for their new colonies in the Americas. Although slavery was not new to Africa and some kingdoms flourished because of it, the slave trade caused great human suffering and distorted local economies. Before this trade ended in the nineteenth century, more than ten million Africans had been enslaved and taken from the region, while slave raiding and slave wars became commonplace.

Despite great resistance by its inhabitants, by 1914 all of West Africa except Liberia was under European colonial rule. European colonization greatly affected West Africa, setting the modern political bounderies and molding the region's economies into their present dependence on the export of raw materials rather than processed goods. By the 1970s, West Africa was independent again but as nineteen nations that had little relevance to ethnic groupings or historical African states.

Geography

Bordered on the north by the Sahara Desert, on the east by the highlands of Cameroon, and on the west and south by the Atlantic Ocean, West Africa forms a natural geographical region. It can be categorized into four regions: the Sahara, the Sahel (a semidesert strip south of the Sahara), *savanna*, (grasslands with scattered trees and shrubs), and forests. Other features include the major rivers (Niger, Benue, Senegal, Volta, and Gambia) and the mountains and highlands such as the Jos Plateau in Nigeria and the Futa Djallon in Guinea.

Only the southern part of the Sahara falls into West Africa, and this occupies a broad belt of the region's northernmost lands. Blazing hot in the day and surprisingly cold at night, the Sahara is virtually uninhabitable except for a few *oases* (fertile pockets) fed by underground springs. In particular, large parts of northern Mauritania and Mali fall into this region. The Sahel is basically the semidesert region that separates the Sahara from the savanna regions to the south. Vegetation is sparse and there are periodic *droughts* (periods of inadequate rainfall). The savanna lands are characterized by open wood and grasslands. They form the largest of the four regions and separate the Sahel from the forest lands. The dense, tropical forests are scattered along the south-facing coastline of West Africa. Liberia and Cameroon are the most densely forested West African countries. Both the savanna and the forests have rainy and dry season cycles. The rains fall heaviest and for longest in the forests, giving rise to the term *rainforest*.

People today

The population figures provided for each people are estimates from between 1980 and 1996. The ethnic groups selected for inclusion tend to be distributed across more than one country. It is difficult, therefore, to use national censuses (which may vary in frequency and amount from nation to nation) to gather up-to-date information about a people's numbers. Statistics have been taken instead from a variety of sociological and anthropological sources, they have been included only to indicate the size and relative importance of an ethnic group.

The vast majority of West Africans are Black Africans. A considerable minority, however, are not. The Moors of Mauritania, for example, are of mixed Arab, Berber, and Black African descent. Through migration, conquest, and intermingling over the years, the people of West Africa have diversified into many different ethnic groups. It is difficult, therefore, to classify people according to physical appearance or race. Also, national boundaries were colonial inventions and do not relate to ethnic groups or historical African states. Ethnic groups are more a matter of cultural, linguistic, historical, religious, and perceived similarities than race or nationality.

Hundreds of languages are spoken in West Africa. Many are particular to certain ethnic groups, while others are widely spoken due to historical factors. Arabic and Hausa are used widely, as they were important

© DIAGRAM

trading languages. Also, Muslims often learn Arabic, the language of the Islamic holy book, the *Koran*. English and French have been used in West Africa since the colonial era. The result of this diversity is that many West Africans can speak more than one language.

There are also many religions in West Africa. The bulk of these are particular to certain ethnic groups. The two most widely practiced religions in West Africa, however, are Islam and Christianity. At least 900 years ago, Islam was introduced from North Africa, primarily as a result of trading across the Sahara. In the nineteenth century, Christianity was brought to West Africa by European missionaries. Today, many Christians and Muslims combine the beliefs and practices of an African religion with their belief in Islam or Christianity.

Lifestyles

The population of West Africa is roughly seventy-percent rural. This statistic hides a huge variety of lifestyles. Many people are farmers; others are traders, scholars, weavers, doctors, artists, writers, teachers, miners – there are as many occupations as you would expect to find in any contemporary society. It is difficult, therefore, to describe the typical lifestyle of any specific group of people.

To some extent, geography determines the lifestyle of agricultural peoples. In the desert regions, *nomadic* lifestyles have evolved to make it possible to live off almost barren land. Nomads travel with their herds in search of water and pasture in the desert and semidesert regions. Apart from desert and semidesert regions, most West African soils are capable of *subsistence agriculture* at least, enabling farmers to only provide for the immediate, day-to-day needs of their families. Until recently, the most common system of agriculture was *shifting cultivation*. A patch of land is cleared, cultivated, and then abandoned when exhausted. In the forest regions, this is combined with a technique called *slash and burn* to clear the land of its cover. Although labor intensive, such methods are ideally suited to the tropics. They allow the soil to recuperate, conserve the environment, and the burning of vegetation fixes nutrients in the soil.

Recent changes

Agriculture has undergone many changes in West Africa. Larger farms, plantations, cash crops, and *monoculture* (one-crop) farming systems are all relatively recent changes. They have had both positive and negative effects. Cash crops for export such as coffee, cacao (cocoa beans), *groundnuts* (peanuts), and timber bring welcome foreign currency into many West African countries. Dependency on exports of raw materials rather than processed goods, however, leaves economies at the mercy of changes in the world market. This is why West African countries have tried to develop other sources of income and establish manufacturing and processing industries. Furthermore, soil erosion was not a problem historically as indigenous farming methods protected the fragile topsoil. Intensive farming techniques have changed this. Soils not given time to recuperate become increasingly poorer and the loss of natural vegetative cover has left them vulnerable to erosion. *Deforestation* in the forest regions has had a similar effect.

Since the 1960s, the Sahelian countries have suffered from increasingly frequent droughts. Inadequate rainfall and the overuse of the fragile semidesert lands that fringe the Sahara have turned patches of land into desert or less productive land – a process called *desertification.* Desertification is partly caused by climate and partly by people. Governments encourage nomads to settle down so that they are easier to control and, combined with pressure on the land to produce more crops (for both an increasing population and a growing cash economy), these have worsened the process of desertification.

West Africa is rich in mineral deposits such as oil, gold, diamonds, natural gas, and phosphates. Some, such as gold and diamonds, have long been mined in West Africa; others, such as oil and phosphates, have only recently been exploited. Nigeria is now one of the world's leading petroleum producers.

A growing urban population has been a part of all these changes. *Urbanization* is not foreign to West Africa. The Yoruba people, for example, have lived in towns for hundreds of years, and many busy modern cities are based on ancient trading centers. The pace of urbanization, however, has increased markedly as more and more people migrate from rural areas in search of better prospects in the cities. This has put more pressure on rural areas to feed the growing cities, while the lack of employment in urban areas has meant the development of an urban poor. Conversely, *underemployment* (although few people are totally unemployed many do not have enough work to provide for all their needs) has led to thriving, urban informal sectors in which people create their own job opportunities – by illicit trading, for example. These so-called "black markets" are an important source of income to many urban West Africans.

Asante

he Asante (or Ashanti) mostly live in the forest
regions of south-central Ghana and are the largest
ethnic group in that country. A number also live in
the neighboring states of Togo and Ivory Coast. There are
probably 1,500,000 Asante.

T he Asante (or Ashanti) mostly live in the forest
regions of south-central Ghana and are the largest
ethnic group in that country. A number also live in
the neighboring states of Togo and Ivory Coast. There are
probably 1,500,000 Asante.

History

The Asante are descended from people who settled in
West Africa thousands of years ago. A number of small
groups of Akan-speaking peoples, including the Asante,
settled in the forest regions of modern Ghana between the
eleventh and thirteenth centuries.

ASANTE EMPIRE The separate Asante chiefdoms were
united by Osei Tutu in the 1670s, when he took the title of
asantehene (king) and founded the Asante Empire. Osei
Tutu fell in battle in 1717 and was succeeded by Opoku
Ware, who continued the Asante expansion. By the time
of his death in 1750, the Asante Empire was the largest
and most powerful state in the region. Much of the Asante
success lay in the strength and flexibility of its fighting
units and battle formations. Its wealth and prosperity was
based on mining and trading in gold and trading in slaves,
with both the Europeans who visited the coast (which

Asante timeline

1000s– 1200s	Early Akan-speaking peoples settle forests of modern Ghana
1640	Fante states emerge on coast.
1670s	Asante united by Osei Tutu; Asante Empire founded
1717– 1750	Under Opoku Ware, empire becomes most powerful in region
1816	Asante defeat Fante states
1824	First Anglo-Asante War
1826	Second Anglo-Asante War
1863	Third Anglo-Asante War
1874	Fourth Anglo-Asante war: Asante Empire in disarray
1883– 1888	Civil war as Asante Empire begins to disntegrate
1888	Agyeman Prempe I attempts to revive Asante Empire
1896	Prempe exiled by British; colony established over Asante
1900	Asante rebel against British
1902	British annex Asante territories to Gold Coast colony
1954	National Liberation Movement (NLM) formed in Asante region
1957	Gold Coast gains independence as Ghana; nationalization begun
1960s	Many large, mechanized, state-run farms created
1966	Military coup in Ghana
1969	Return to civilian rule in Ghana
1979	Military coup led by Jerry Rawlings forces elections
1981	Military coup led by Rawlings ends civilian rule in Ghana
1983	Process of denationalizing some state enterprises begins
1992	Elections end military rule; Rawlings is elected president

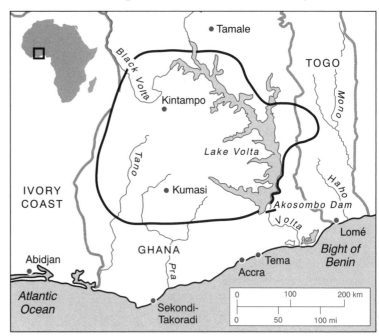

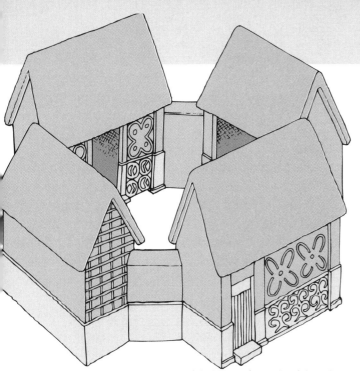

Asante architecture

Until relatively recently, Asante dwellings were usually constructed of four linked huts around a courtyard. The walls had a wooden framework and were built up with mud. The sides of the huts facing the courtyard were often left open or partly open. The outside walls were decorated with elaborate and beautiful relief patterns. Roofs were usually thatched. Many dwellings now have brick or concrete walls and roofs of sheet metal.

Royal musicians

These musicians are blowing side-blown ivory horns at an Asante state ceremony. These horn blowers play an important part at any major event; every regional chief has his own blower who follows him, sounding his horn in the distinctive notes that identify each particular chief.

came to be known as the "Gold Coast") and with other African kingdoms to the north of the Asante Empire.

At its height under Osei Bonsu (who ruled 1801–24), the Asante Empire covered all of modern-day Ghana as well as parts of Togo, Burkina Faso, and Ivory Coast. The Fante people on the Gold Coast were conquered by 1816. This brought the Asante increasingly into conflict with the British, who wanted to control the gold trade. The result was a series of Anglo-Asante wars. In the first, in 1824, the Asante defeated the British; in the second, in 1826, the Asante were defeated, but the British did not pursue their victory. In 1863, the Asante twice defeated joint Anglo-Fante troops. When Asante troops crossed the Pra River in 1874 – to reconquer the Fante – they were driven back by the British, who invaded the Asante capital, Kumasi, and blew up the royal palace, leaving the empire in disarray. Agyeman Prempe I became asantehene in 1888 and began reuniting the Asante; nervous of his success the British forced him into exile in 1896 and declared the Asante Kingdom (Prempe never recovered the full empire) a *protectorate* (colony). A further war followed in 1900, led by the *ohemmaa* (most senior woman). Despite great resistance, the Asante were defeated and the British annexed their lands in 1902.

Sword

This Asante sword has a gold-plated wooden hilt, a rounded pommel and a decorated blade. Swords such as this are used for ceremonial purposes – they are carried in front of processions and state funerals.

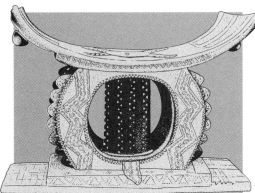

Silver Stool *(above)*

This wooden stool, which is decorated with silver sheeting, was made for the most senior Asante woman – the *ohemmaa*. When a new asantehene is selected, the ohemmaa inaugurates the selection in her capacity as owner of her own Silver Stool.

Gold-weights

Brass weights used to measure gold dust or nuggets have been made and used by the Asante for centuries. They are generally accurate to 0.2 oz (0.5 g). The weights were produced using the *lost-wax* or *lost-beetle* methods of casting.

Language

The Asante language is also called Asante and is a dialect of Twi – one of the Akan group of languages.

Ways of life

Most Asante people make their living as farmers. Cash crops are grown as well as crops such as rice and yams for food. The most important cash crop is cocoa, Ghana's chief export. Other crops grown include coconuts, kola nuts, and palm kernels (seeds). Mining of diamonds, gold, bauxite, and manganese provides employment for some Asante; still others work in forestry. In urban areas, many Asante are employed in business or work for the government as civil servants. Producing wood carvings for the tourist trade is a source of funds for some Asante.

Social structure

POLITICAL STRUCTURE In the nineteenth century, the asantehene Osei Tutu introduced the Golden Stool, declared to embody the soul of the Asante nation. It symbolized the political unity of the Asante and was never sat on. The British attempted to confiscate the stool, so it was kept in hiding for many years. Its remains have been incorporated into a new stool, which is still a potent symbol of Asante unity today. The Asante Kingdom is now part of modern Ghana. Although the asantehene is still an important figure in Ghanaian society, his role is now largely ceremonial and symbolic.

Culture and religion

RELIGION Most Asante people are either Christian or Muslim. The Asante royalty, however, still follow the Asante religion as part of their role in maintaining Asante culture. It involves the worship of a supreme god called *Nyame,* who communicates through various lesser gods.

METAL CASTING The Asante are famous as the producers of probably the most beautiful goldwork in Africa. To this day, Asante state ceremonies and celebrations are occasions for a show of gold regalia worn and used by the Asantehene and his chiefs, all devised as symbols of their political and moral authority. Asante goldsmiths and other metal workers use a casting technique called the *lost-wax* method. The flourishing of representational forms of brass gold-weights – used to measure gold dust and nuggets – from the 1700s onward was, in part, allowed by the use of this effective method. Small, intricate pieces as well as larger, simpler pieces can be produced by lost-wax casting.

First, a wax model is made of the object to be cast. Modern metal casters usually use purified beeswax. The model is then covered with a clay mold in which a hole is pierced. When the mold is heated, the wax melts and is poured out of this hole. Molten metal is then poured into the cavity. After the metal has hardened and cooled, the mold is broken and the casting is removed for polishing and perhaps further decorative work. A possibly older method of metal casting is the *lost-beetle* method. The technique is the same as for lost-wax casting except a real object such as a beetle, seed, or flower is encased in the mold. When heated, the object in the mold turns to ash.

WEAVING The Asante are famous for weaving the colorful *kente* cloth, from which the national dress of Ghana is made. Kente cloth is distinctive for its complex patterns.

© DIAGRAM

Asante battle formation (above)
Asante battle formation was a precision instrument that few enemies resisted successfully. In outline, it bore a striking resemblance to a modern airplane. At the "nose" is a party of scouts; the "fuselage" is made up of a column of warriors, followed by the Commander-in-Chief and his military staff; the "tail" section comprises a rearguard; and the "wings" consist of five columns of men each. At the rear of each wing is a group of medical personnel – rather like wing flaps. This awesome arrangement of men was the secret of the Asante Empire's military success.

Gold pendant
The Asante are masters of gold working, not surprisingly since they have been mining and trading gold for centuries. This gold pendant is exquisitely decorated and comes from the royal regalia of the *asantehene*.

Bambara and Malinke

T he Bambara (or Bamana) and the Malinke are the two main subgroups of the Manding peoples (also called Mandinka or Mandingo). The Bambara people live chiefly in the grasslands around Bamako in the upper Niger River region of southern Mali. The Malinke have tended to settle more wooded areas, and now live largely in Mali, Guinea, and the Ivory Coast. Many also live in Gambia, Senegal, Guinea-Bissau, and Burkina Faso. There are approximately 2,500,000 Bambara and 1,500,000 Malinke people.

History

All Manding peoples originate from a mountainous region of the same name that sits astride the border of Guinea and Mali. This area was the base of the vast medieval Empire of Mali. In 1235, Sundiata – the Muslim ruler of the Malinke Kingdom of Kangaba – won a decisive battle against the leader of the Susu, Sumanguru, who ruled the region at that time. Malinke settlers and troops pushed west to the Atlantic, and the Empire of Mali came to

Bambara and Malinke timeline	
c. 750	Malinke Kingdom of Kangaba established
1100s	Islam introduced to Kangaba
1235	Sundiata founds Empire of Mali
1240s	Expansion of Empire of Mali
1312– 1337	Mali reaches height during reign of Mansa Musa
1324	Mansa Musa travels to Mecca
c. 1490	Mali Empire eclipsed by Songhay Empire
c. 1550	Mali ceases to exist
c. 1740	Bambara found state of Segu
1754	Kaarta founded by Bambara
c. 1800	Dyula kingdom of Kong south of Segu is a rich trading empire
1850s– 1860s	Muslim Tukolor Empire conquers Kaarta and Segu
1870s– 1880s	Samori Toure founds the Second Mandinka empire
1890s	Mandinka Empire relocates in east to resist French
1898	French conquer Mandinkas
1958	Guinea independent, with Sekou Touré as president
1960	Mali independent, with Modibo Keita as president
1960s– 1980s	Recurring *drought* causes famine in Sahelian countries
1968	Moussa Traoré takes power in military coup in Mali
1977	Keita's death in detention leads to widespread popular unrest
1979	Traoré elected president
1991	Traoré overthrown in coup
1992	Alpha Konare elected president of Mali
1994	*CFA franc* devaluation causes widespread hardship

control one of the largest-ever West African realm. Fertile soils, gold mining, ironworking, and trade led Mali to prosperity. Under Mansa Musa in the 1300s, Mali reached its height. After his death in 1337, Mali began to disintegrate and by the 1400s, it was no longer important. In c. 1490, Mali's power was eclipsed by the dominant Songhay Empire and by c. 1550 it had ceased to exist.

The Bambara founded the upper Niger state of Segu (based around modern Ségou) in 1600, which reached its peak between 1740 and 1800. In 1754, the Bambara founded the state of Kaarta (based around modern Nioro du Sahel) to the west of Segu. These were the strongest states in the region by 1800. In the mid-nineteenth century, a Dyula man (part Malinke, part Bambara in origin) called Samori Toure attempted to revive the medieval Empire of Mali. By 1881, Toure had established a huge empire in West Africa covering much of the present-day nations of Guinea and the Ivory Coast as well as southern Mali. It took the French seven years to defeat Samori Toure's empire; but, by 1898, the Second Mandinka Empire (as it was called) had fallen. By 1900, European colonial powers controlled the whole region.

RECENT EVENTS In the 1950s, one of West Africa's most important nationalist leaders was a descendant of Samori Toure – Sekou Touré, who lead the bitter struggle for Guinean independence from the French. In 1958, Guinea became the first French West African nation to achieve independence, with Sekou Touré as prime minister.

Language

The Bambara and Malinke speak different dialects of Manding, which is a Mande language.

Antelope dance
Two masked youths jumping like antelopes perform a *Tyi-wara* dance. Tyi-wara is a mythical half-man, half-antelope attributed with the introduction of cultivation to the Bambara. The straight-horned headress depicts a female; the maned, curved-horned headdress a male. Until recently, Tyi-wara dances were performed to make the crops grow, to celebrate a harvest, or to praise the best farmer. The dances are still performed, but with the onset of Islam and changing farming techniques they are becoming less common.

Malinke town
Round houses with mud walls and thatched roofs form the Malinke town of Kirina, near Ségou in Mali. The barrel-like structures are grain stores. Hundreds of years old, Kirina is where the famous battle that lead to the foundation of the Empire of Mali was fought between Sundiata and Sumanguru in 1235.

© DIAGRAM

Figurine
Malinke female figurines like this one are more naturalistic and less geometric than their Bambara counterparts. The artists who carved them were usually blacksmiths.

Musical history (*below*)
A twenty-one-stringed harplike instrument called a *kora* accompanies a Malinke *dyeli* (bard) as he sings and recites stories from Manding history.

Ways of life

FARMING The Malinke and Bambara are mostly farming people, although many now live and work in towns. They grow corn, millet, and sorghum and also keep cattle, though milking cows was probably introduced from outside Manding culture.

TRADE Trade has always figured strongly in both people's economies. Products such as rice, corn, and cloth are sold, while butter, milk, livestock, and salt are bought. Islamic traders of mixed Malinke and Bambara ancestry have long dominated the southern end of trans-Saharan commerce. They are still active traders in much of West Africa today. Indeed, their dialect has become an international language of trade. These people and their language both go by the Mande name of "Dyula," which literally means "trader."

Social structure

From early times, Manding villages have been grouped into distinct units. A group of Bambara villages formed a district overseen by a *fama* (leader) who was drawn from a dominant family. A group of Malinke villages would make up a *kafu* with its own king or *mansa*. Bambara and Malinke families are also organized into *dyamu.* This is the Malinke word for groups of people who share the same name, male ancestors, and *taboos* – for instance, a ban on eating the animal that a dyamu has as its totem. Two famous, noble Malinke dyamu are the Keita and Traoré families. Both the founder of the Empire of Mali, Sundiata, and the first president of the Republic of Mali, Modibo, were Keitas, while the second president of Mali, Moussa, was a Traoré. There are also *nyamakala,* which are basically craft or profession groups. There are nyamakala for people such as *dyeli* (bards), farmers, leatherworkers, and blacksmiths. A system of "secret" societies helps to regulate how people live their lives. For example, *ntomos* prepare young boys for *circumcision* and initiation into adult society. Joining such societies and obeying their rules and taboos helps to make people conform to what are considered acceptable kinds of behavior.

Culture and religion

RELIGION Islam is now the main faith of both the Bambara and Malinke. It was introduced to the Malinke Kingdom of Kangaba in the 1100s by Berber traders from North Africa. Almost all the Malinke adopted Islam, but the Bambara gave up their old beliefs and rituals more slowly.

MUSIC Music has long played an important role in Manding culture. Dyeli sing of the deeds performed by the heroes of ancient Mali. Salif Keita is one internationally famous Manding singer who follows this tradition – updating it with topical references. Many dyeli accompany themselves on stringed instruments called *koras* or the three-stringed *kontingo*. Also used are gourd harps called *bolombatos*; *ngonis* – four-stringed lutes once played by Bambara musicians to inspire men to fight; and *balafons*, wooden percussion instruments similar to xylophones.

TEXTILES Bambara women are famous for their dresses of cloth decorated with abstract patterns depicting symbolically important animals such as lizards, tortoises, and crocodiles. In the past, most Bambara men would wear *mud cloths*, distinctive for their light patterns on dark backgrounds. Women design these cloths by an elaborate process using mud, ash, and soap.

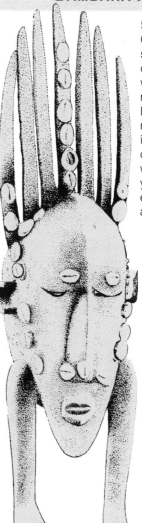

Standing mask
Cowrie shells and stylized horns ornament this wooden "standing mask" of the Bambara. Such masks figure in the intiation ceremonies of *ntomo* societies, which prepare young boys for entry into the adult community.

Mud cloth *(left)*
Bambara *mud cloths* are traditionally woven by men but bear geometric designs applied by women. The designer starts by soaking the cloth in water colored with crushed leaves or bark. This dyes the cloth brown or black. Next, she paints a pattern onto the cloth with mud. When this is dry, the artist repaints the pattern in a soap made from ash and vegetable oil. Then she applies more mud to the pattern. When the cloth is dry, the mud is scraped off, the dye beneath comes off as well, and the pale pattern is exposed. The linear shapes at the top of this cloth represent crocodiles.

© DIAGRAM

37

Four medieval empires

Three empires in turn dominated West Africa from the 300s to the late 1500s: Ghana, Mali, and Songhay. A fourth empire, that of Kanem-Borno, lay farther east. Ghana and Mali are known as the Empire of Ghana and the Empire of Mali to distinguish them from the present-day states with the same names. For more than a thousand years, these empires flourished and grew wealthy by trading in gold and salt. Most of what we know about them comes from West African oral history and accounts written by travelers and traders from North Africa, such as the Arab geographer Al Bakri in the 1060s and the Moroccan explorer Ibn Battuta, who visited Songhay and Mali in the 1300s.

Empire of Ghana

The Soninke people were the citizens of historic Ghana. They are a present-day people and speak a language also called Soninke, which belongs to the Mande language group. Present-day Soninke people live in Senegal. A Berber family, the Maga, were probably the founders of Ghana in c. 300. The empire was called Wagadu by its people. In the 500s, the Soninke overthrew the Maga. The despotic king of this empire was called the ghana (war-chief), and other peoples began to use the title of the ruler as the name of the empire.

Ghana lay to the north of the Senegal and Niger rivers, in what is now western Mali and southern Mauritania. Its capital, Kumbi Saleh, lay southwest of Timbuktu (modern Tombouctou). It was a twin city. One part was a stone-built Muslim town, with a dozen mosques (Muslim houses of worship) and 20,000 inhabitants. This was the commercial center, where Berber traders brought fabrics, manufactured goods, and food to exchange for gold and salt. It also became a center for the spread of Islam, which was introduced in the 1050s. The other part of the town was where the ghana lived, and he made sure that Soninke religion and ways of life prevailed there.

Medieval Ghana's sources of power and prosperity were the gold and salt trades. For much of its timespan, the state controlled the West African ends of the trans-Saharan trade routes. Some of Ghana's gold came from goldfields to the south, outside the empire's nominal borders, but the Soninke themselves mined most of it. Ghana remained powerful until 1076, when Islamic invaders from the north overran it. It regained its independence after about ten years, and until the 1200s, was the richest country in West Africa. The king kept a large standing army with archers and cavalry to protect it. After 1200, invasions by the Susu people greatly weakened the empire. Ghana lingered on until 1240 when it was taken over by the Empire of Mali.

Empire of Ghana
This map of the Empire of Ghana shows its territories in c. 1000, toward the end of its era of power. Kumbi Saleh was the capital and Walata, Timbuktu, and Audaghost were major trading centers.

Senegal
Audaghost • Walata Timbuktu
Kumbi Saleh •
Nioro •
Gambia
Niger
• Jenne
Kangaba •
Volta

☐ Empire of Ghana
c. 1000

⬭ Goldfield

0 200 400 km
0 100 200 mi

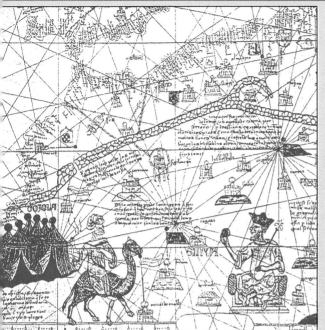

Mansa Musa on his throne
The first European map of West Africa was drawn in 1375 and depicts the Malian king, Mansa Musa. Mali's fame had obviously spread far around the world. Musa is holding up a large gold nugget as if to trade with the Arab merchant who is riding on a camel toward him.

Empire of Mali
Medieval Mali was based on the smaller Kingdom of Kangaba, which was close to and dominated by historic Ghana. Kangaba was founded in c. 750 by the Mande-speaking Malinke people. In 1224, the Susu – a people now living in Guinea and Sierra Leone – overran Ghana, and six years later they invaded Kangaba. The invaders put to death all of the ruling family of Kangaba except for one crippled

prince, Sundiata, who they thought would not be a threat. This was their mistake. Sundiata was a great hunter and a good soldier; he became known as the "Lion of Mali." Sundiata built up his forces, and in 1235 defeated the Susu. By 1240, he had also conquered what was left of the Empire of Ghana, and the Empire of Mali came into existence.

The empire gradually expanded, and by the 1330s it extended to the Atlantic coast covering present-day Senegal, Gambia, Guinea-Bissau, most of modern Mali, parts of Mauritania, and even southern Algeria. It controlled three major trading points, Niani on the upper Niger River (now known only as ruins); Jenne (modern Djenné in Mali); and the legendary, desert-city of Timbuktu. The major sources of Mali's wealth were control of both the gold-trade routes and the goldfields of

Great Mosque of Djenné (below)
This *mosque* in Djenné built earlier this century, stands on the same site as the original mosque built when the city was part of medieval Mali in the thirteenth century.

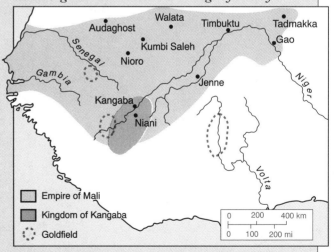

Empire of Mali (above)
This is a map of Mali in c. 1335, two years before the death of its most powerful ruler, Mansa Musa. By this time, Mali had reached its greatest extent.

Bambuk, Bure, and others on the Volta River and in the forests of modern Ghana.

The last, and most, powerful ruler of medieval Mali was Mansa Musa. A devout Muslim, he went on pilgrimage to Mecca in 1324, taking with him a huge quantity of gold. He stopped in Egypt on the way and gave away and spent so much gold that its price fell sharply, with disastrous effects on Egypt's currency. After he died thirteen years later, the Empire of Mali began to disintegrate. By c. 1490, Mali was no longer politically important and by c. 1550 it had been completely absorbed by the Songhay Empire.

Songhay Empire

Songhay was originally a small state founded by the Songhay people in c. 750. It lay on the Niger River across an important trade route, with its capital at Gao. About 1240, the Mali empire absorbed Songhay, but it regained its freedom by the 1340s. Songhay rose to greatness during the 28-year reign of Sunni Ali (reigned 1464–92). He began by seizing Timbuktu from the Tuareg, who had wrested it from Mali. Four years later he captured Jenne. By the time of his death in 1492, Sunni Ali had made Songhay the

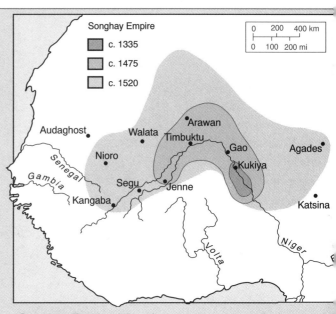

Songhay Empire (above)
Above is a map of Songhay in c. 1515, during the reign of Askia Muhammad. Under this king, Songhay reached the height of its power and took over much of historic Mali's former territories.

Tomb of a mighty ruler
The tomb of Askia Muhammad of Songhay still survives. This is a view of the exterior.

Sankoré Mosque
The Sankoré Mosque in Tombouctou was built by the Muslim kings of Mali. It became the center of Islamic worship during the era of the Songhay Empire, and West Africa's first university was established within its walls. It is built of mud bricks and is the oldest surviving *mosque* in West Africa.

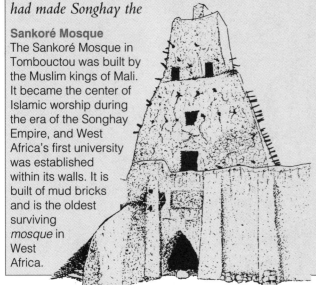

most powerful empire in West Africa. Songhay reached the height of its power during the reign of Askia Muhammad (1493–1528). He was a devout Muslim, and he organized his large empire into provinces, each with a governor. Through military might and religious zeal, Songhay remained powerful until 1591, when Moroccans conquered it. In 1618, the Moroccans set up a puppet state, governed by the rulers of Timbuktu. This state lasted until 1787, when the Tuareg conquered it. Today, about 800,000 Songhay people still live in southern Mali. Their language, also called Songhay, is used by traders over a large area of West Africa.

Kanem-Borno

The empire of Kanem-Borno lay to the northeast of Lake Chad. According to tradition, an Arab leader, Dugu, founded Kanem in c. 800. His descendants ruled the land until 1846. Their dynasty was known as the Sefawa, after Dugu's grandfather, Sayf b. Dhi Yazan – a hero credited with freeing the Yemeni in southwest Asia from foreign rule. The people they ruled over in Africa were the Kanembu, an originally nomadic ethnic group who spoke a language called Kanuri. Their descendants live in Chad, Niger, and Nigeria today.

Kanem became a wealthy empire because of its control of trade routes. It exported ivory, slaves, and gold and imported salt, copper, tools, and horses. By 1150, Kanem was an Islamic state. During the 1200s, it expanded to the north and west and by 1230 Kanem had reached its greatest extent.

Borno was at first a province of Kanem, but in the 1300s nomadic invaders forced the Sefawa to flee from Kanem to Borno, southwest of Lake Chad, and Borno was established in 1386. By the 1500s, Borno had become the dominant power, and Kanem became a province of Borno in 1526. The empire of Kanem-Borno became a center of Islamic civilization. After the collapse of Songhay in 1591, Kanem-Borno became the most powerful empire in sub-Saharan Africa. From 1671, however, the empire began to decline. Much territory was lost in the 1700s and 1800s to the Tuareg people in the north and the Fulani people in the south. Kanem-Borno lasted until it was invaded by the Darfurian slave trader Rabih b. Fadl Allah between 1892 and 1893.

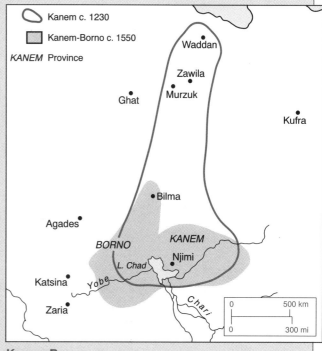

Kanem c. 1230
Kanem-Borno c. 1550
KANEM Province

Waddan
Zawila
Ghat · Murzuk
Kufra
Bilma
Agades
BORNO *KANEM*
Njimi
Katsina · L. Chad
Yobe
Zaria
Chari

0 ———— 500 km
0 ———— 300 mi

Kanem-Borno

Above is a map showing the empire of Kanem in c. 1230 and Kanem-Borno in c. 1550. In 1230, Borno was still just a province of Kanem, which had reached its greatest extent. After being ousted from Kanem, by 1550 the rulers had regained a lot of their old territories from their new base in Borno. The Kanem-Borno Empire reached its height after the collapse of Songhay in 1591.

Borno royal procession

A nineteenth-century engraving depicting the processsion of a sultan of Borno through one of the regional capitals.

Dogon

The Dogon of central Mali live in remote, rocky ravines along a 120-mile (190-km) stretch of the Bandiagara Cliffs and on the *savannas* (grasslands with scattered trees and shrubs) on the plateaus above and below. Although there are fewer than 500,000 Dogon, their culture is significant for many reasons; in particular because they were isolated from neighboring peoples and relatively free of outside influences until quite recently.

History

Very little is known of Dogon history before they came to settle in the Bandiagara region. The Dogon believe that ancient human bones and wooden sculptures found in caves suggest that more than 2,000 years ago the Bandiagara Cliffs were inhabited by a people called the Tellem. Because most of the wood carvings have been dated as no more than 200 years old, however, and because stylistically they resemble modern Dogon work, archeologists believe the sculptures were made by Dogon artisans and that the oldest "Tellem" skeletons probably date from no earlier than the eleventh century.

Cliffside village *(opposite)*
This distinctively Dogon village clings to cliffs that can reach as high as 600 ft (180 m) above the plain below.

Dogon timeline

1240	End of Dogon vassalage to the Empire of Ghana
1307–1332	Dogon driven westward to Bandiagara Cliffs by Mossi
1359	Mossi invade Empire of Mali
c. 1490	Mali's power eclipsed by dominant Songhay Empire
1898	French conquest of Soudan
1960	Soudan wins independence from France as Mali
1960s–1980s	Recurring *drought* causes famine in Sahelian countries
1962	Mali leaves the *African Franc Zone* and adopts the new Malian franc as currency
1968	Lieutenant General Moussa Traoré takes power in bloodless military coup
1977	Modibo Keita's death while in detention leads to widespread popular unrest
1984	Mali reenters African Franc Zone and readopts *CFA franc* as currency
1991	Traoré overthrown in bloodless coup
1992	Democratic elections end military rule in Mali
1994	CFA currency devalued by fifty percent; demonstrations break out as Malians experience economic hardships

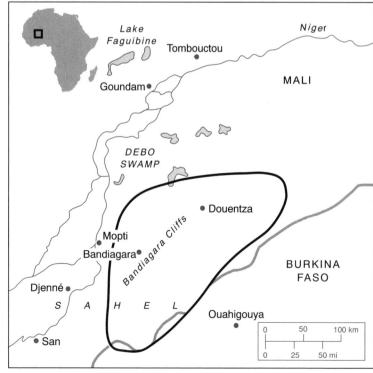

© DIAGRAM

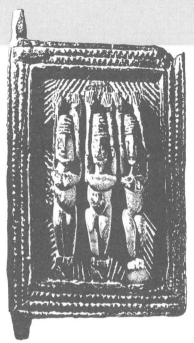

Granary door *(above)*
This wooden door from a *granary* (grain store) is decorated with figures of Dogon women. The zigzag patterns represent the style in which the universe was created as well as the union of man and woman. In recent decades, most such decorative features have been removed from buildings for sale to art collectors or ethnologists.

The Dogon say their ancestors fled from the southwest to the Bandiagara Cliffs from the thirteenth century onward to escape conquest by the medieval empires of Ghana, Mali, and Songhay. The isolated and inhospitable terrain also proved to be excellent protection from attacks by neighboring Mossi and Fulani peoples – in particular during the eighteenth- to nineteenth-century period of *jihads* (Islamic holy wars) against non-Muslims such as the Dogon. The cliffs made access difficult, while the land itself was considered to be of little value by outsiders.

Language
The Dogon language is also called Dogon.

Ways of life
Despite rocky terrain and minimal rainfall, many Dogon are farmers. Terraces have been created on the slopes to enable crops to be grown. Soil, compost, and bird droppings are gathered from cliffside ledges and spread on the terraces. Millet is the main crop, but sorghum, other grains, vegetables, fruit, and cotton are also cultivated. Families keep sheep, goats, and hens, and where sufficient land is available, cattle and donkeys are raised. Generally, women sow, weed, and harvest grain while the men clear land and fertilize the crops. Water has always been precious, and *droughts* from the 1960s to the 1980s led to hundreds of deaths and thousands of Dogon left the region. Today, many young men leave their villages to work in the cities of Mali and Ivory Coast, sending most of their wages home to their families in Bandiagara.

Ginna house
Dogon villages are often clustered around a *ginna* (or "great house"), which is occupied by the most senior man. The small compartments are used to store religious artefacts.

Social structure

VILLAGES AND HOUSES The most characteristic Dogon villages are those on the sides of the Bandiagara Cliffs or beneath them, where the Dogon live in small villages of under 1,000 people. Each village is made up of one or more extended families who trace their descent from a common male ancestor from father to son. These *lineages* are headed by the oldest man, who lives in the *ginna* (or "great house"). In villages of only one lineage, this man will also be the village head. Several villages are often grouped around a well or waterhole.

In these villages, the people live in small rectangular mud houses. Tall towers made of rock or mud and with thatched roofs, once used as *granaries* (grain stores), now provide general storage. Houses and granaries may be joined together with mud walls to form family *compounds*. The most important public building is the *togu na*, an open-sided building on the main square, which is used by men for village council meetings.

Dogon social organization and architecture are closely related to Dogon beliefs. The layout of buildings, both individually or collectively, is seen as symbolic of complex aspects of the Dogon religion that may also be expressed by the human form. The Dogon often use the human body as a metaphor for both society and religion. For example, houses and villages are ideally built on a north-south axis to resemble a prostrate being; the togu na represents a man's head; and a house can symbolize the union of man (ceiling) and woman (central room) as well as Heaven (roof) and Earth (floor). The position of buildings is symbolic of how *Amma* (God) made the world and provides a link between the Dogon and their ancestors.

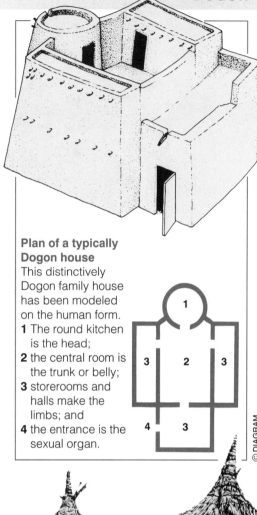

Plan of a typically Dogon house
This distinctively Dogon family house has been modeled on the human form.
1 The round kitchen is the head;
2 the central room is the trunk or belly;
3 storerooms and halls make the limbs; and
4 the entrance is the sexual organ.

© DIAGRAM

Granaries
The design of these *granaries* (grain stores) is inspired by the sheer cliff faces and rocky outcrops of Bandiagara. Few granaries are used to store large amounts of grain now, as most is taken to market.

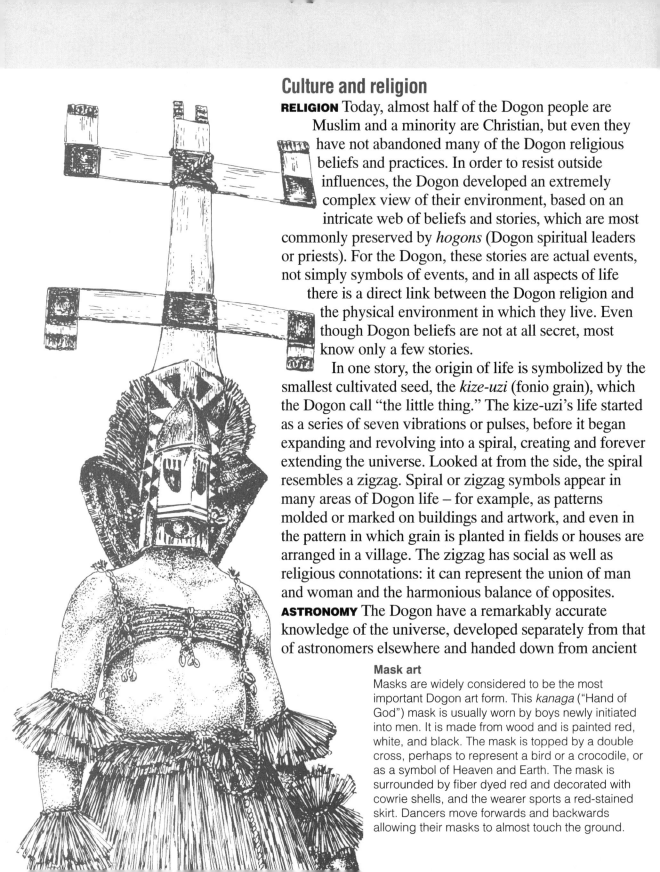

Culture and religion

RELIGION Today, almost half of the Dogon people are Muslim and a minority are Christian, but even they have not abandoned many of the Dogon religious beliefs and practices. In order to resist outside influences, the Dogon developed an extremely complex view of their environment, based on an intricate web of beliefs and stories, which are most commonly preserved by *hogons* (Dogon spiritual leaders or priests). For the Dogon, these stories are actual events, not simply symbols of events, and in all aspects of life there is a direct link between the Dogon religion and the physical environment in which they live. Even though Dogon beliefs are not at all secret, most know only a few stories.

In one story, the origin of life is symbolized by the smallest cultivated seed, the *kize-uzi* (fonio grain), which the Dogon call "the little thing." The kize-uzi's life started as a series of seven vibrations or pulses, before it began expanding and revolving into a spiral, creating and forever extending the universe. Looked at from the side, the spiral resembles a zigzag. Spiral or zigzag symbols appear in many areas of Dogon life – for example, as patterns molded or marked on buildings and artwork, and even in the pattern in which grain is planted in fields or houses are arranged in a village. The zigzag has social as well as religious connotations: it can represent the union of man and woman and the harmonious balance of opposites.

ASTRONOMY The Dogon have a remarkably accurate knowledge of the universe, developed separately from that of astronomers elsewhere and handed down from ancient

Mask art

Masks are widely considered to be the most important Dogon art form. This *kanaga* ("Hand of God") mask is usually worn by boys newly initiated into men. It is made from wood and is painted red, white, and black. The mask is topped by a double cross, perhaps to represent a bird or a crocodile, or as a symbol of Heaven and Earth. The mask is surrounded by fiber dyed red and decorated with cowrie shells, and the wearer sports a red-stained skirt. Dancers move forwards and backwards allowing their masks to almost touch the ground.

times. For example, the Dogon know of Sirius A – the brightest star in the sky – and also of Sirius B, some 100,000 times less bright and impossible to see with the naked eye. Furthermore, the Dogon know that it takes fifty years for Sirius B (which they call "the smallest thing there is") to orbit Sirius A, and they have inherited from their ancestors a deep understanding of other characteristics of the stars and universe.

Dogon woman (left) Both Dogon men and women trade at the local markets. Pottery and spinning are largely done by women, while men practice weaving and basketry.

Rainmaker (right) This painted wooden figure is one of many ancient works kept in Dogon *granaries* (grain stores). They are used in rainmaking: the open hand brings the rain and the closed hand stops or prevents it.

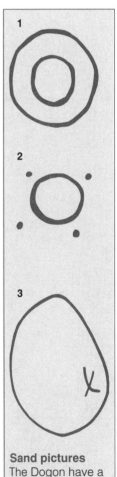

CAVES Along the Bandiagara Cliffs are numerous caves, many of which are used by the Dogon as cemeteries. Dogon sculptures (as well as those supposedly made by the "Tellem" people) are found in difficult-to-reach caves, some of which are no more than niches along the sheerest of the cliffsides. Even today, Dogon people keep their most important masks and statues hidden in secret cliffside caves, occasionally removing them for religious ceremonies and festivals. Because of theft by outsiders for sale as works of art, sculptures are often defaced by the Dogon to reduce their value to others and prevent their removal by antique hunters or art dealers.

Sand pictures
The Dogon have a wide knowledge of astronomy. These pictures drawn in the sand depict:
1 Saturn's halo;
2 the four moons of Jupiter; and
3 the orbital path of the star Sirius B.

© DIAGRAM

Food and drink

West African food and drink vary enormously, a reflection of the region's varied geography and cultural diversity. Over a period of centuries, the West African diet has been influenced by contact with other parts of Africa, North and South America, and Europe; while the region has contributed greatly to the creation of cuisines elsewhere, in particular those of the Caribbean, Brazil, and the American South.

In rural areas, most families grow much of their own food. Staples vary according to local climatic and soil conditions, but rice is widely available. It is, however, fairly expensive because much that is consumed is imported. In areas with sufficient rainfall, cassava, yams, and other root vegetables as well as plantains are key cooking ingredients, while in the semidesert Sahel, couscous (made from coarse-ground semolina or other grains) is popular. Vegetables too are varied, and include the leaves of sweet potatoes, pumpkins, cassava, and other plants used to create spinachlike dishes, and beans, peppers, eggplant, and okra. Sauces for vegetable and meat dishes are often based either on groundnut *(peanut) paste or on palm oil. Food is typically eaten from a communal dish with the fingers, though in strict Muslim households, men and women often eat out of separate dishes.*

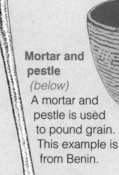

Mortar and pestle *(below)*
A mortar and pestle is used to pound grain. This example is from Benin.

Basket bowl *(above)*
Baskets are commonly used as containers for food. some baskets are so tightly woven that they can hold liquids, such as palm wine.

Cassava balls
Cassava can be pounded, then mixed into a paste and made into balls. The balls are fried and eaten with stew.

Common vegetable plants

1 Cassava is originally from South America, but it now grows widely in West Africa, probably having arrived with slave ships. The large, coarse tubers (root vegetables) are boiled and usually pounded into a white, pastelike, substance. A coarse flour is also produced and the plant's leaves are an important vitamin source.

2 Yams are very large tubers that are produced in wet, southern areas, especially in Nigeria. The white or yellow flesh and the leaves are prepared in a similar way to cassava. Much valued commercially, yams are important to many peoples.

3 Cocoyams (also known as taro or dasheen) are similar in appearance and use to cassava and yams but are considered tastier. Cocoyams require considerable rainfall and are therefore grown mainly in wet, forested areas.

Meat and Fish

Both meat and fish form central parts of meals, though many households find their cost prohibitive except for festivals and other special occasions. On the coast, people fish in the Atlantic, but the region's rivers – in particular the Senegal, Niger, and Benue – are important sources of freshwater fish. Today, fish is often frozen, but it is also sun-dried or smoked for ease of storage and transportation, and because these forms are essential ingredients for many recipes. Mutton and goat are the most commonly consumed meats, with beef and chicken reserved for special occasions because they are expensive. Game is a staple in many areas, but overhunting and loss of habitat have resulted in limited availability. Rodents and antelopes are much sought after, but monkeys, snails, cats, and dogs are also sometimes hunted.

Alcoholic drinks

A wide variety of alcoholic drinks is produced in West Africa, though many Muslims in the region do not consume alcohol. A traditional drink that is popular in coastal areas is palm wine: a white, frothy brew made from the naturally alcoholic sap of the species of palm tree that also provides palm nuts and palm oil (used for cooking and frying).

Beer is the most popular alcoholic drink, and cassava flour, millet, sorghum, and corn are used in the fermentation process of homemade brews. Today, however, Western-style beers are also produced in virtually every country, often using a mix of imported hops and locally grown cereals or cassava. Nigeria has the largest range of commercially produced beers, with both light and dark varieties popular.

4 Millet is a grain that can be grown in the Sahel because it requires little rainfall. it is used for porridge and beer.

5 Sorghum is also known as guinea corn and has a cornlike appearance. Sorghum requires more rainfall than millet, but it withstands *drought* well and is used in similar ways.

6 Corn is produced in areas of moderate to heavy rainfall and is eaten either on the cob or is used to make flour.

7 Okra (or gumbo) is a vegetable native to West Africa. The pods are used in many soup or stewlike dishes as they have a thickening effect

8 Plantains are widely produced in West African areas with heavy rainfall and are fried, boiled, or dried to be made into a flour.

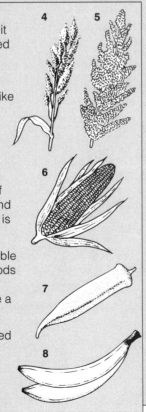

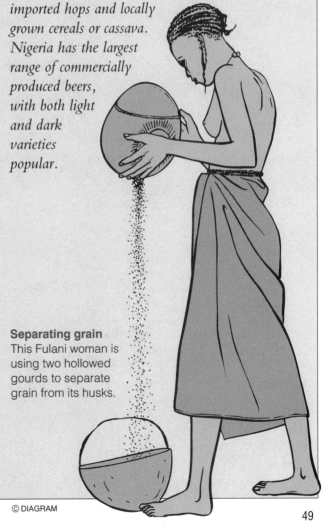

Separating grain
This Fulani woman is using two hollowed gourds to separate grain from its husks.

Ewe

he Ewe mostly live in lands along the southern end of the border between Ghana and Togo. The Ewe are closely related to the Fon. There are probably over one million Ewe in Togo and over two million in Ghana. There are four main groups: the Ewe "proper," who live in Ghana and southwest Togo; the Anlo Ewe, who live in Ghana west of the River Volta; the Watyi, who live in southeast Togo; and the Mina, a small group living on the Togo coast. A few Ewe also live in Benin.

History

According to Ewe oral history, the Ewe migrated to their present lands from what is now Benin and Nigeria in the mid-1600s. For many years, the coastal Ewe traded with Europeans, at first selling war captives as slaves and – when the slave trade ended – selling raw materials such as *copra* (the dried "meat" of coconuts) and palm oil.

COLONIALISM In the late 1800s, the western Ewe came under British colonial rule in what was then called the Gold Coast, while the Germans ruled the eastern Ewe in German Togoland. After World War I, Togoland became a

Ewe timeline

c. 1650	Ewe migrate westwards from present-day Nigeria and Benin
1784	Ewe at war with the Danes settled in forts on coast
1807	Britain abolishes slave trade
1874	British establish Gold Coast
1884	German Togoland colony established
1914– 1918	World War I. Ewe caught up in fighting between British and Germans
1954	Togoland Congress founded with the aim of reunifiying Ewe land and people
1957	Ghana independent
1960	Togo independent
1963	Military rule begins in Togo
1966	Military rule begins in Ghana
1969– 1972	Brief period of civilian rule in Ghana
1976	In Togo, General Etienne Eyadéma leads military coup
1979	In Ghana, Flight Lieutenant Jerry Rawlings forces elections
1981	Rawlings takes power in military coup in Ghana
1991	Widespread civil unrest in Togo; transitional government is set up and opposition parties are unbanned
1992	Rawlings is elected president in Ghana. 200,000 refugees flee disturbances in Togo; many die during presidential elections; Eyadéma remains as president
1994	Togolese opposition narrowly wins legislative elections

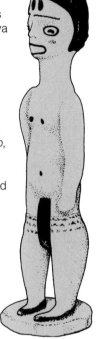

Akple (left)
An Ewe woman prepares a mix of corn and cassava flour to make *akple*, a staple food eaten with meat or vegetable stew.

Tro sculpture (right)
This wooden sculpture is of an unidentified Ewe *tro*, (spirit or deity). The Ewe religion involves the worship of a supreme god called *Mawu*. The Ewe believe that Mawu can only be approached through the *trowo* (the pural of tro). Each tro is worshipped by specific groups, or "cults."

joint British and French *protectorate* (colony). When the Gold Coast was about to become independent as Ghana in the 1950s, some Ewe in Togoland voted to join Ghana. The rest are now in independent Togo.

Language

The Ewe people speak the Ewe language, which has several dialects. The Anlo Ewe dialect has become the main literary language of the Ewe.

Ways of life

FARMING AND FISHING The Ewe are mainly farmers, growing food crops for their own needs, such as cassava, sorghum, corn, millet, yams, and pulses, and cash crops such as onions, shallots, palm oil, and cacao (cocoa-beans). They keep cattle, sheep, and goats. On the coast fishermen make large catches, especially of anchovies. The Ewe fish from canoes or from the shore, using large nets that require fifty men to haul them in. People also catch fish in the rivers and lagoons that dot the coast.

TEXTILE INDUSTRY Spinning thread and strip-weaving blue and white cloth are ancient crafts among the Ewe. Strips only a few inches wide are woven and then sewn together to make wider fabrics. It is still partly a cottage industry (a

Strip-weaving (below)
Many Ewe weavers use hand looms to weave strips of cloth that can be sewn together to make larger pieces of cloth. Each strip is roughly 5 in. (12.5 cm) wide.

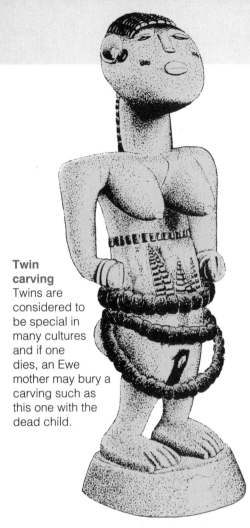

Twin carving
Twins are considered to be special in many cultures and if one dies, an Ewe mother may bury a carving such as this one with the dead child.

Independence celebrations (*below*)
This strip is one of a collection woven to celebrate the independence of the Gold Coast as Ghana in 1957. The inlay picture depicts the inkpot and pen used to sign the Instrument of Independence. This representational style is more typical of modern Ewe weaving than the more stylized, traditional designs.

small-scale business operated from workers' homes), but in the towns there are now many small textile factories. Blue was for a long time the only dye easily made fast, but since other colors have become available the Ewe have incorporated them into their designs.

TRADE Along with their Fon counterparts, Ewe women have a virtual monopoly over the trading economies of the coastal ports and markets. Acting as both wholesalers and retailers, they buy and sell a wide variety of items from imported cloth to foodstuffs or trade beads.

Social structure

SOCIAL STRUCTURE Ewe society is organized around *lineages,* or extended families. Members of the same lineage share a common ancestor traced from father to son – usually a grandfather of up to eight generations ago. The head of the lineage is the oldest male. Traditionally, the lineage's ancestral land was considered a gift to unborn descendants and could never be sold. In a system where the lineage group provided for all the needs and welfare of its members, selling land was not wise. The growth of a cash economy, however, and the resulting increased production of cash crops has changed this. In many areas, land is now bought and sold and people depend less on their lineage groups for their livelihoods.

POLITICAL STRUCTURE Lineages are important politically as well as socially. In the past, the head of the founding lineage of a village was considered the leader, or *dufia*. He had an advisory council of village elders – both male and female – to help him make decisions. In turn, a council of dufias would advise the overall leader of a whole region or *dukowo,* of which they were ten. These dukowo were politically independent but culturally united.

The imposition of colonial rule disrupted the political organization of Ewe society. Leaders who had resisted the colonialists were replaced. These new leaders often had their own interests at heart and not those of the group. Furthermore, the Ewe no longer had the right to oust rulers who abused their positions, as they had in the past.

Lineage heads still function politically, but many of their roles are now performed by the government. For example,

Keta cloth
Strip-woven cloth that uses contrasting colors between *warp* (lengthwise threads) and *weft* (threads that go across the warp), and usually with inlaid designs, is called *keta*. Keta shares many similarities with the cloth called *kente,* which is produced by the Asante people of Ghana.

Keta wrapper
This Ewe man is wearing a wrapper made from *keta* cloth. Wrappers are wide pieces of cloth made from many strips sewn together. The cloth is wrapped around the body and tucked in at the waist.

the dukowo head of the Anlo Ewe, the *awoamefia*, is the final judge of cases involving customary law. Criminal matters, however, are dealt with by the state judiciary.

Culture and religion

RELIGION Today, nearly half of the Ewe people are Christians. The Ewe religion is still widely practiced, at times in conjunction with Christianity. In fact, new traditions have developed that incorporate the two religions. For example, on the death of a lineage member one soul (the "life-soul") is considered to return to God for judgment. This is according to the Christian tradition. The person's "personality-soul," however, returns to the ancestral lineage in *Tisiefa* (the "Other World"). This is according to the Ewe religion.

DRUMS AND INSULTS Drumming is at the heart of Ewe festivals. The Ewe call all performances "drums," and their repertory includes dancing, drama, composing and performing poetry, sculpting, and singing. One of the oldest Ewe drums is called *kpegisu* and was probably originally a war drum. A typical performance starts with a new song. The composer holds a *havalu,* a session in which he teaches the new song to his fellow drummers. The havalu is followed by a general singing practice for everybody, known as *hakpa.* A feature of some gatherings is a *halo*, an exchange of insulting songs between villages.

© DIAGRAM

53

Slavery and the slave trade

In the early sixteenth century, European colonists in the Caribbean and Central and South America forced Native Americans and European convicts to work their mines and plantations. Most of these unwilling workers died of disease and cruel treatment, so the settlers turned to Africa to solve their labor needs, believing that Africans could best withstand the harsh working conditions and tropical climate. The Spanish and Portuguese were the first to enter the Atlantic slave trade, but by the late sixteenth and early seventeenth centuries many other European nations had established forts and trading posts along the coast of West Africa from present-day Senegal to Angola. By the time the slave trade was finally halted in the late nineteenth century (over fifty years after it was banned by Britain in 1807 and the United States in 1808), over ten million African men, women, and children had been transported across Atlantic.

Slavery existed before the European arrival in Africa, with prisoners of war, debtors, or criminals being common victims of enslavement. Slavery and slave trading had never been practiced on such a large scale before, however, nor with such a disregard for human suffering. The introduction of material incentives – goods exchanged for slaves – resulted in the established rules governing enslavement breaking down, and "wars" were provoked to legitimize kidnapping. Most slaves originated from relatively

Loading the ship (right) This old engraving depicts slaves being loaded onto a ship for transportation, probably to the Americas.

Below deck (below) The cramped conditions of a slave ship are shown in this drawing of the floor plan below deck.

short distances from the coast and few peoples were left unaffected by the trade; local economies were distorted and social relationships undermined.

Factors, or resident agents, dealt with local rulers through a web of European and African traders who would skim off a proportion of the goods traded. Slave purchasers developed preferences for particular parts of Africa and crude ethnic stereotypes evolved. For example, the Akan peoples of Ghana were regarded as being rebellious in nature; the Igbo of Nigeria were considered easy to control though prone to moodiness or even suicide; and the Manding peoples from Senegal were seen as excellent house servants. Goods such as iron bars, guns, beads,

NORTH
AMERICA

SOUTH
AMERICA

Africa in the Americas
The tinted areas of the map show where slaves were taken in the Americas. Today, African influences are unmistakable throughout the Americas. Rarely is it possible for individuals to trace their lineage to any particular African people, but contemporary diet, religion, music, language, and folktales often bear witness to a rich African heritage. In Brazil (the most important destination for slaves), African influences are clear, for example, in the rituals of the Candomblé religion, in which the gods are clearly Yoruba derived.

Key dates

1517	Spain officially approves importing of African slaves to the Caribbean, disregarding the Pope's disapproval
1593	The Netherlands starts to establish trading posts along the coast of West Africa
1600s	England, France, Denmark, the Netherlands, Portugal, Spain, and Sweden engaged in the Atlantic slave trade
c. 1750s	The Atlantic slave trade reaches its peak with Africans being shipped to the Americas at a rate of around 100,000 per year
1700s	Opposition to slavery and the slave trade develops in Europe and the United States
by 1804	States north of Maryland abolish slavery
1787	Freetown (Sierra Leone) founded by British philanthropists as a settlement for liberated African slaves
1791	Slave revolt in Haiti leading to independence from France in 1804
1807	Britain prohibits slave trade in its colonial possessions
1808	United States prohibits slave trade
1833	Britain abolishes slavery throughout its empire
1847	Liberia founded by the American Colonization Society as a settlement for liberated slaves
1865	The defeat of the Confederacy in the American Civil War; slavery abolished throughout the United States
1888	Slavery abolished in Brazil

cloth, and alcohol were traded. In 1756 it was recorded that one man could be traded for 115 gal. (435 l) of rum, and a woman 95 gal. (360 l).

The triangle trade

Most slave ships sailed from European ports carrying goods to trade for African slaves. Slaves were delivered to trading posts and crammed into the ships' holds without delay because ships' crews feared falling prey to fever or dysentery that resulted in a life expectancy of just two years for European residents of West Africa. On board the ships, conditions were appalling with little ventilation, poor food, and no medical care. In general, up to one quarter of the Africans died (and sometimes more) during the three- to six-week journey as a result of disease, suicide, or by being thrown overboard for acts of resistance or because of sickness. On arrival in the Americas, the Africans were sold and the ships were loaded with gold, silver, sugar, tobacco, cotton, and other goods. The ships then returned to Europe, unloaded, and resumed their triangular trading. This trade was also carried out by a smaller number of American slavers who crossed the Atlantic carrying rum, returning to America via the Caribbean.

NORTH
AMERICA

EUROPE

Tobacco, cotton, sugar, molasses, gold, silver

Atlantic
Ocean

Manufactured goods

AFRICA

WEST
INDIES

Slaves

SOUTH
AMERICA

© DIAGRAM

Fon

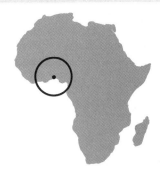

The Fon live in the Republic of Benin, the former Kingdom of Dahomey. Culturally, especially in terms of religion, the Fon have much in common with the neighboring Ewe people of Togo and Ghana. Today, there are approximately two million Fon.

History

At its peak the Fon Kingdom of Dahomey had a population of only a quarter of a million people. The concentration of people and the relatively short distances between the main centers of population, however, helped to permit highly centralized rule. Ruled by a strong king and administered by officials in an efficient bureaucracy, the Fon created one of West Africa's most powerful nations, successfully resisting European control until the end of the nineteenth century.

THE RISE OF THE KINGDOM OF DAHOMEY The original inhabitants of what was to become the Kingdom of Dahomey lived in small and scattered groups, with no overall loyalty to a king. Nominally subjects of the Yoruba, individual villages and towns jealously guarded their own independence, but whenever possible sought to extend their influence over weaker neighbors. Up to the beginning of the seventeenth century, the states that were

Fon timeline

1625	Fon kingdom founded at Abomey
1708–1732	King Agaja's reign sees Fon expansion to create Dahomey
1728–1729	Oyo invades Dahomey and exacts tribute
1729	Dahomey capital is transferred to Allada
1818–1858	Under King Ghezo, Dahomey begins to free itself from Oyo
1858	Under King Glele, Dahomey
1889	is fully independent again
1883	French take Porto-Novo
1889	King Behanzin tries to drive French out of Dahomey
1892	French conquest of Dahomey
1960	Dahomey wins independence
1972	Major Mathieu Kerekou seizes power in miitary coup
1974	Dahomey adopts Marxism-Leninism (communism)
1975	Dahomey renamed Benin
1989	Benin abanbons Marxism-Leninism
1991	Nicéphore Soglo elected president in first democratic elections
1992	Widespread persecution of Kerekou's supporters
1994	Widespread unrest and economic hardship after CFA franc is devalued by fifty percent
1996	January 10 designated a national holiday in honor of Fon (Vodoun) religion

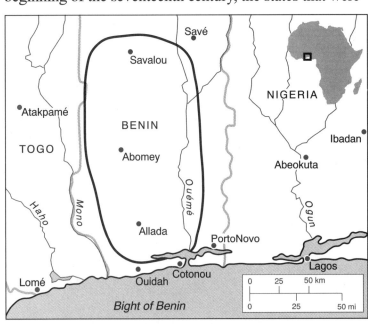

emerging were all small, though some were beginning to gain greater significance.

The foundations of the Fon kingdom were laid in the early seventeenth century, when a group of warriors from Allada gradually gained control of much of the interior as far north as where present-day Abomey is located. At Abomey, the first ruler of the new Fon kingdom built his palace on the grave of the local king he defeated, establishing a tradition followed by future kings. The charismatic King Agaja, remembered as a great statesman, reigned from 1708 to 1732 and greatly extended the kingdom.

The Kingdom of Dahomey was one of Africa's few states to maintain an army, which increased from about 3,000 soldiers in the early eighteenth century to 12,000 in the mid-nineteenth century. It included up to 2,500 ferocious female warriors – women dedicated to the personal protection of the king. Arms obtained from European traders enabled the Fon to extend their territories. Controlling the coast allowed the Fon to have greater control over the profitable slave trade and to protect their own people from capture and sale. Fon ports along what was known as the "Slave Coast" became important points on the so-called triangular trading route that linked Europe with Africa and the Americas. In the late eighteenth century, for example, the port of Ouidah was recorded as receiving each year forty to fifty Dutch, English, French, and Portuguese ships importing arms and other goods and exporting slaves.

THE FALL OF THE KINGDOM OF DAHOMEY
After the end of the slave trade in the early nineteenth century, palm oil became Dahomey's key export activity. Falling oil prices weakened Dahomey's economy, however, and the French – who had greater military might – seized control of the coast by 1889. In despair the king, Glele, committed suicide and was succeeded

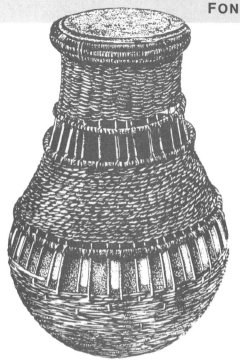

Burial drum *(above)*
This type of clay and raffia drum, called a *kpezi*, would have been part of a Fon funeral ceremony. The dead would have been buried with many pieces of pottery.

Art for art's sake
In Fon society, brass castings of animals and people – such as this figure of a man using a hoe – have long been produced without any religious or ceremonial functions, but purely as ornamental objects of beauty and as symbols of the wealth of their owners. Today, brass casting continues, but mostly for the tourist trade. Other arts for which the Fon are renowned include wood carvings and decorative textiles.

© DIAGRAM

by his son Behanzin. Despite the fierce resistance of King Behanzin and his armies, Dahomey was conquered in 1892, and the French then employed local chiefs to help administer their new territory.

Dahomey became independent in 1960, and in 1975 it changed its name to the Republic of Benin, marking the end of its association with France.

Language

The various Fon dialects belong to the Kwa language group of the Niger-Kordofanian family.

Ways of life

FARMING Historically, the Fon had a wide range of crops, many of which were introduced from the Americas and Asia. Intensive farming remains the primary way of life among the Fon, but cash crops such as palm oil (used for cooking and frying) and cocoa are also grown today. Chickens, sheep, goats, pigs, and cattle are also kept.

HOUSING Traditional housing compounds are *wattle-and-daub* structures (made of interwoven twigs plastered with mud), with houses arranged around a courtyard in which are placed altars to gods.

Social structure

SOCIAL STRUCTURE The Fon social structure is based on the *clan*, members of whom are related through their male ancestors and live together in the clan's own *compounds* within a larger town or village. The children of a marriage are usually considered to "belong" to the father's family and clan. In some cases, however, the children are considered part of their mother's family. This often happens when a man marries a woman without paying her family *bridewealth,* a payment to seal the alliance.

POLITICAL STRUCTURE In the past, absolute power was invested in the king, but administration was extremely complex. It was organized on strict military lines, often for clear military purposes. For example, agriculture was carefully regulated to control how much grain and other crops would be produced each year and to reserve proportions for the army. The king was treated with great awe, and those approaching him had to lie on the ground

Reliefs
A collage of animals and weapons decorate this wooden door from a royal palace in Abomey, the former capital of the Kingdom of Dahomey. The animals shown – the snake and the chameleon – figure in many West African legends.

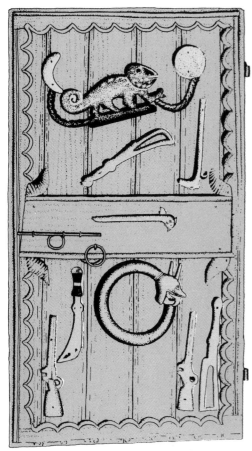

Appliqué cloth (left)
This banner uses brightly colored *appliqué* (cutout shapes applied to a contrasting background) to depict a lion hunt. This technique has long been used for religious images, banners, and chiefs' headgear. Today, such appliqué work continues as an important art form, with clothes produced for tourists but often also bearing illustrations that feature social commentary.

and throw dust on themselves as an acceptance of their lowly status. The king would choose one of his sons as heir, with the rest of the royal family kept powerless to reduce chances of a coup.

Local chiefs achieved their positions of power through acts of courage rather than through birth, while the king always appointed commoners as ministers. There was a strict hierarchy of male ministers, all with clearly defined functions, and each had a female equivalent who officially took precedence over him just as, technically, the king was outranked by the *queen mother*.

Culture and religion

RELIGION Most follow the Fon religion, which closely resembles the Ewe religion, though some Fon (especially along the coast) have adopted Christianity. The Fon creator-god *Mawa* is usually seen as female, but has both male and female traits. Mawa causes coolness at night and is associated with the Moon, peace, fertility, gentleness, and rain. She gave birth to a son, *Lisa*, the Sun god who causes the day and its heat and represents strength and endurance. Mawa and Lisa are generally seen as the rulers of all the other gods, who represent earth, sky, thunder, and knowledge, for example. The Fon call their gods *vodun* (singular *vodu*).

King Behanzin as a shark
This painted, wooden figure shows a fusion of man and shark, representing King Behanzin. Fierce animals, most commonly the leopard, are often used as symbols for depicting African rulers.

© DIAGRAM

59

Fulani

Fulani warriors
Although guns were available in West Africa during the eighteenth- to nineteenth-century period of *jihads* (Islamic holy wars), the Fulani jihadists disdained to use them, considering them fit only for slaves. The Fulani shown here were part of the cavalry.

The Fulani are one of the largest ethnic groups in West Africa totaling about twenty-three million. They are widely dispersed throughout West Africa and have large groups in Senegal, Gambia, Guinea, Mali, Burkina Faso, Niger, Nigeria, Cameroon, and Chad. Smaller groups live in most other West African states. One group, the Bororo, are found in the semidesert Sahel region of Niger and northern Nigeria. Small numbers of Bororo are also found in Chad and Cameroon.

The Fulani are known by a number of names. They call themselves "Fula." The Hausa people know them as "Fulani" (singular, "Fula"), a name that has been adopted by others. In some French-speaking countries, such as Senegal, they are called "Peul" (singular, "Pullo").

History

The Fulani are descended from both North Africans and sub-Saharan Africans. The earliest Fulani were *nomadic* cattle herders, who traveled great distances with their herds in search of water and pasture. Although the existence of the Fulani has been known for more than a thousand years, their origins are unknown. One theory is that they originated in East Africa, migrated northward through Sudan and Egypt, then turned westward along the Mediterranean coast to Morocco. It is known, however, that from Morocco, the Fulani moved southward into

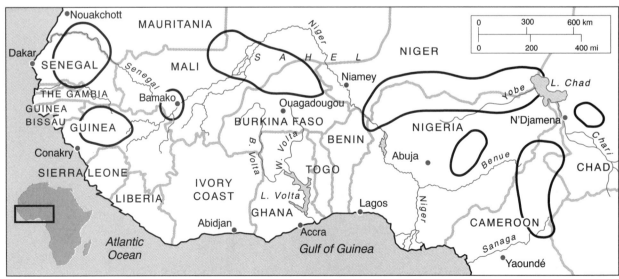

High-class Fulani woman
The huge rings dangling either side of this Malian woman's face are attached to her hair, not her ears, and they are solid gold. She is of the upper classes, and these rings probably represent much of her family's wealth.

Fulani timeline	
700s–1400s	Fulani migrate southward and eastward from present-day Morocco and Mauritania
1650	Muslims migrate into Futa Toro and Futa Djallon
1673	Unsuccessful Fulani *jihad* (Islamic holy war) in Futa Toro
1725	First successful Fulani jihad launched in Futa Djallon
1775	Second,successful, Fulani jihad launched in Futa Toro
1800	Fulani Islamic jihad states of Futa Toro, Futa Djallon, Wuli, and Bundu in existence
1804–1809	Fulani jihad in Hausaland led by Usman dan Fodio; Sokoto Caliphate established
1827	Independent Islamic state of Macina established
1830	Sokoto Caliphate reaches greatest extent
1852	Al Hajj Umar declares jihad in Futa Toro; Tukolor (Fulani) Empire established
1862	Macina conquered by Tukolor Empire
1893	French defeat Tukolor Empire
1903	British defeat conquer the Sokoto Caliphate
1950–1970s	West African states become independent
1960s–1980s	Recurring *drought* (period of inadequate rainfall) causes famine in Sahelian countries
1994	Widespread unrest and economic hardship in *African Franc Zone* after *CFA franc is* devalued by fifty percent

what is now Mauritania from the 700s. The cradle of the group in West Africa is in northern Senegal, where they settled in Futa Toro, a state founded by the ancestors of today's Tukolor Fulani people. Some Fulani also moved farther southward and eastward, settling in the Futa Djallon region of Guinea and also in northern Nigeria.

In the 1670s, the Fulanis began a series of *jihads* (Islamic holy wars) against their non-Muslim neighbors, which lasted for almost the next two centuries. During this period Futa Toro, Futa Djallon, Wuli, and Bundu (the latter another Tukolor-founded empire) were established as jihad states. The most significant was the Sokoto Caliphate founded by a Fulani Muslim scholar named Usman dan Fodio. In the late eighteenth century, he rose to power in northern Nigeria, where the Fulani shared territory with the Hausas. In 1804 he was elected "Commander of the Believers," and proclaimed a jihad. Within twenty-five years, he had established an Islamic Fulani-Hausa empire – the Sokoto Caliphate – in northern Nigeria and parts of what are now Niger, Benin, and Cameroon. He handed over the government of this

© DIAGRAM

Fulani states and migrations

The Fulani have been in West Africa for centuries. They have long been settled in areas such as Futa Toro and Futa Djallon, which at times formed independent states.

Key

1 **Fulani migrations 700s–1400s**
➤ Migration route
▨ Empire of Mali c. 1350

2 **Islamic (Fulani jihad) states and migrations c. 1650–1800**
➤ Migration route
▨ State c. 1800

3 **Fulani jihad states and Tukolor empire 1860**
▨ Fulani state
▨ Jihadist empire of Al Hajj Umar (Tukolor Empire)

4 **Fulani states and Tukolor Empire 1885**
▨ Fulani state
▨ Tukolor Empire
⬚ French colonial expansion

A Futa Toro
B Wuli
C Bundu
D Futa Djallon
E Macina
F Sokoto Caliphate

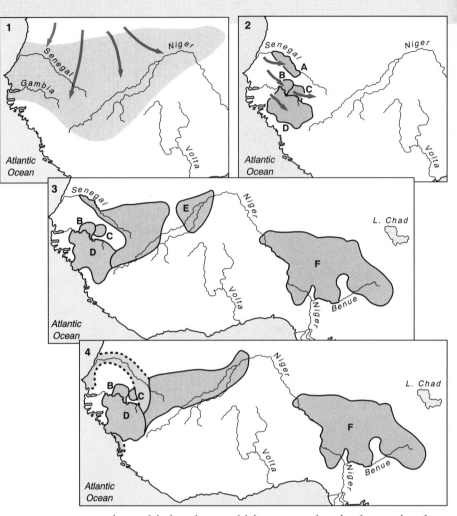

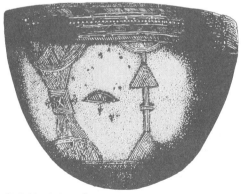

Calabash bowl
Bowls like the one below are made from dried *calabashes* (a calabash is a type of gourd). They are often elaborately decorated and have multiple uses.

empire to his brother and his son, and retired to a simple life of teaching and writing.

As a result of the Fulani conquest of Hausa territory, in northern Nigeria today many Fulani people live in the same villages as Hausa people. There is some intermarriage, and many Fulani living among Hausa have adopted the Hausa language and customs. Although the Fulani are in the minority among the Hausa, historically the Fulani have been the ruling aristocracy.

Language

The Fulani language is called Fulfulde. It belongs to the West Atlantic group of the Niger-Congo language family. A characteristic of Fulfulde is that singular and plural nouns begin with different consonants and have different suffixes, so singular and plural words often appear and sound quite different. There are a number of different dialects of Fulfulde. In northern Nigeria, where the Fulani and the Hausa peoples share territory, about half the Fulani now speak Hausa. A few Fulani have moved east into Sudan, where they are neighbors of Arab cattle herders; these Fulani have adopted Arabic.

Ways of life

There are several groups of Fulani, and this diversity reflects a range of occupations and ways of life. Most Bororo Fulani are *seminomadic pastoralists* (livestock raisers), living in the *savannas* (grasslands with scattered trees and shrubs) and the semidesert Sahel with their herds. The Wodaabe are a related Fulani group in northeastern Nigeria numbering only about 45,000; they are also largely cattle-keeping pastoralists. The Fulbe n'ai are also pastoralists, but grow crops as well as herd cattle. The Fulbe sire are former pastoralists who have lost their cattle through *drought* (periods of inadequate rainfall) or disease and have had to settle as farmers or market gardeners; they are usually quite poor and are often disliked by other Fulani groups. The approximately half-a-million Tukolor (or Toucouleur), living mostly in Senegal, are chiefly farmers and fishers. Although they have been linked with the Fulani for several centuries, their origins are separate and some consider the Tukolor a separate ethnic group. Finally, there are the Toroobe, many of whom belong to the professional classes. Toroobe people are often teachers, religious leaders, and local government officials or civil servants, forming a wealthy minority who live among the Hausa in the towns and cities.

NOMADIC PASTORALISM The pastoral Fulani are often *nomadic*, moving from place to place with their herds of cattle, sheep, or goats in search of water and pasture. Among the

Long-horned cattle
The cattle of the *pastoral* Fulani are the long-horned zebu breed. They are hardy animals, able to withstand long marches from one pasture to another and can feed on whatever grazing is seasonally available.

Bororo nomad
This man is a Bororo Fulani. Most Bororo are *pastoralists* (livestock raisers) who keep mainly cattle. The lifestyles of many Fulani pastoralists have been drastically altered by the severe *droughts* (periods of inadequate rainfall) of the 1960s to 1980s. Herds were decimated and many people were forced to sell their animals and migrate to urban areas or refugee camps to avoid starvation.

© DIAGRAM

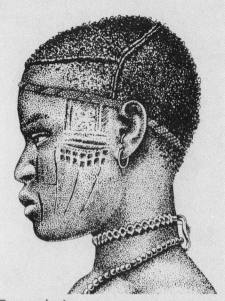

Personal art

A Wodaabe man (*below*) and a Fulani woman (*above*) from Benin illustrate the range of personal adornment adopted by the Fulani. Young Wodaabe men paint their faces at certain festivals and wear elaborately embroidered garments. Some Fulani women use facial tattoos and scars as a way of enhancing their beauty and making themselves more attractive, though this practice is becoming uncommon.

pastoralists the Bororo are notable. Their lives are tuned to the seasons. From October to May is the dry season, when the grass withers and the Bororo stay close to deep wells that do not run dry. In late May, the rains come and the climate is wet until September. The grass grows and grazing is plentiful. Many Bororo have a simple life, making temporary shelters of branches and leaves, or carrying portable huts with them. Their material wants are few: ropes, some tools, cooking pots, mats, and blankets. They make butter, using goatskins as churns, and sell milk and butter at markets or exchange them for other foodstuffs and goods.

In the twentieth century, there has been an increasing trend towards sedentary settlement. Government polices – encouraging nomads to settle down in order to make them easier to govern and tax – and modern international boundaries have restricted the activities of nomads. Increasingly frequent droughts and *desertification* (a type of land degradation) in the fragile Sahel have exacerbated this process. Many Fulani familes are now settled in one place and move their herds from group to group. In fact, the majority of Fulani are now sedentary farmers.

DIVISION OF LABOR In both Wodaabe and Bororo families the women work as hard as the men, if not harder. Their tasks include carrying water from the nearest supply, milking the cows, building and tending the camp fires, and pounding millet into flour to make a kind of porridge.

FARMING The Tukolor, unlike the original Fulani, appear to have been always a settled group, mostly engaged in cultivating field crops and fishing. Muslim since the eleventh century, they migrated in order to spread the Islamic faith, not to seek fresh lands for pasture.

Social structure

Rural households tend to be large and male dominated. A man, his wife or wives, sons, grandsons and their wives and children, make up a typical household. There is a definite class system, with religious leaders holding high status, and artisans and the descendants of former slaves forming the lowest classes. Urban Fulani largely follow the organization of the people who they live among.

MARRIAGE When a Bororo couple have decided on marriage, the man brings a *bridewealth* – often oxen – to the girl's parents. The animals are then used to provide the wedding feast. The giving of bridewealth seals the alliance and is seen as a token of respect. A Bororo man may have more than one wife, providing he is rich enough to support them all. Tukolor males follow the Islamic tradition in being permitted to have more than one wife, but few can afford the bridewealth to do this.

Culture and religion

RELIGION Originally, the Fulani had their own religion. Many converted to Islam in the 1300s, however, particularly those in the east. At first, the Fulani of Futa Toro and Futa Djallon retained their old beliefs and persecuted the Muslims. But both these states were converted to Islam in 1776. Today, the majority of the Fulani are Muslims. One of the most devout groups is the Tukolor, who converted to Islam in the eleventh century. By the mid-nineteenth century, the Tukolor had established a large Islamic empire that eventually extended as far north as modern Tombouctou, Mali.

FESTIVALS AND ADORNMENT Among the Bororo, May is the time for festivals and courting. The young men paint their faces to attract the girls. Among the Wodaabe, the men perform certain dances at the annual *worso* festival, which celebrates marriages and births of the previous year. Two dances dominate the worso – the *yaake* and the *geerewol*. During the yaake dance, the men are judged for charm, magnetism, and personality by elders. Dancers apply pale powder to their faces and black kohl to their eyes to accentuate their features. Hairlines are often shaved to heighten the forehead and a painted line may elongate the nose – attributes considered attractive by the Wodaabe. Geerewol dancers dress in tight wrappers and wear strings of beads and feathered turbans. Singing and jumping at an increasing pace, they are judged for their beauty by young, unmarried women. These dances prove the ability of men to attract women, a particularly admired male attribute. Dancers no longer perform when their eldest son is old enough to compete.

Milk carrier
A young Fulani woman carries a calabash bowl on her head. It contains milk, which is protected by a smaller, upside-down calabash that floats on the milk's surface.

© DIAGRAM

Hairstyling: designs and techniques

Fulani fashions
A Fulani woman from Mali (*right*) wearing an elaborate style that incorporates ring-shaped beads. Many Fulani women wear amber beads or coins worked into the hair. This sometimes signifies that their families are *nomads*, who travel with their herds of animals in search of water and pasture. Fulani men also decorate their hair and even wrap it in gold. This Bororo Fulani man (*below*) has had brass wound around sections of braided hair. The brass must be polished daily to keep it shiny.

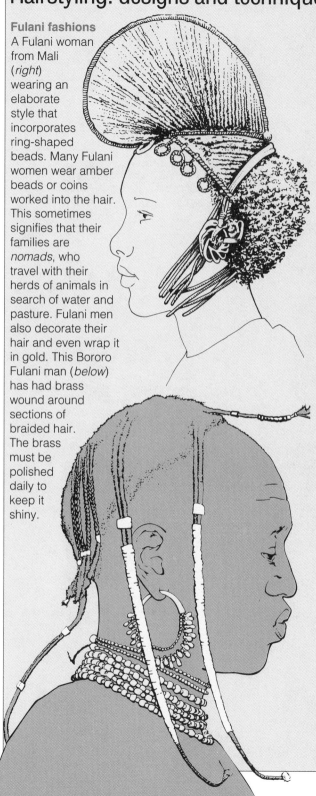

Hairstyling in West Africa is a great art form, and a wide variety of recognizable styles has developed over the years. Many of these styles are still worn today, both in Africa and elsewhere. From the Yoruba, for example, come many styles — using a variety of techniques, alone or combined — that are now fashionable around the world.

Variations

Hair styles vary from region to region and from group to group. Even within one ethnic group many different styles may have emerged. The Fulani, for instance, are scattered over a large part of West Africa, and their hairstyles can vary considerably from one region to aother.

New from old

In the recent past, a certain style signified a time of life or the passing of an important milestone, such as reaching puberty. Some members of a society, such as religious leaders, might wear a particular style to

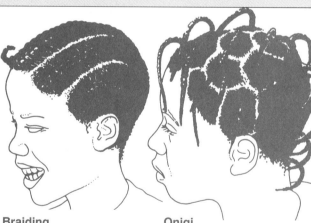

Braiding
Braiding (or cornrowing) is a popular and versatile technique. Another is threading, in which the hair is parted in sections and wrapped with thread, making the strands easier to work into designs that stand away from the scalp.

Onigi
In this design, the hair is wrapped to resemble sticks; the word "*onigi*" means "sticks" in the Yoruba language. It is a relatively simple style to create, and it forms the basis for many of the more elaborate, threaded styles.

signal their important roles. Today, however, hairstyles are chosen more often for their attractiveness rather than for their symbolism. Traditional hairdressing is still common, but new interpretations of old styles are being created, and hairpieces are often added for more dramatic designs. Hair attachments or extensions are often woven into the hair to give a greater choice of style.

Hairdressing stalls

At Igbo markets there is often a hairdressing booth where women can have their hair styled as part of the social event of going to market. For Igbo girls, hair is important in the transition to adulthood. After she begins puberty, an Igbo girl has her hairstyle redone frequently, and each style is often increasingly elaborate.

Kanuri style (*left*)
This Kanuri woman from northeast Nigeria wears a design using braids and, at the top, a cloth wrapping.

Braids (*center left*)
The braids of this Sara woman from Chad are tightly woven near the scalp and looser at the bottom to soften the effect.

Beads (*below*)
Beads are another common accessory in West African hairstyles. Here, beads of different sizes, shapes, and colors have been threaded on to the hair.

Eko Bridge
One of the most widespread of the onigi-based designs is called Eko Bridge. Threaded strands are joined at their ends to form circles, creating a crownlike shape. The design is named for a bridge in Lagos, formerly the capital of Nigeria.

© DIAGRAM

Hausa

The Hausa are the most numerous West African ethnic group, and most of them live in a region known as Hausaland. Although mostly in northern Nigeria, Hausaland extends north as far as the Sahara Desert; to Lake Chad in the east; and to the Niger River in the south. Outside of this region, Hausa people can be found throughout Africa working as traders. There are probably about twenty-five million Hausa.

History

The first Hausa settlements were built during the eleventh and twelfth centuries. By about 1350, many of the cities had developed into independent city-states. The major ones were Kano, Katsina, Zamfara, Gobir, Kebbi, and Zazzau (present-day Zaira). Different city-states were dominant during the various periods of Hausa history. Important trade routes had reached Hausaland from the north by the fifteenth century, and it became known for its cloth manufacturing and dyeing.

The greatest upheaval in Hausa history came at the beginning of the nineteenth century. In 1804, the leader of the Islamic Fulani people – the Muslim cleric Usman dan Fodio – declared a *jihad* (Islamic holy war) against the

Hausa timeline

c. 1000s–1100s	Hausa communities established in northern Nigeria and southern Niger
1350	Hausa city-states emerge
1400s	Islam is introduced to Hausaland via the empires of Mali and Songhay
1804–1809	Hausa states conquered by Fulani leader Usman dan Fodio; Sokoto Caliphate established
1830	Sokoto Caliphate at greatest extent
1903	British defeat Sokoto the Caliphate
1950s	Discovery of petroleum desposits in Nigeria
1960	Niger and Nigeria win independence
1967–1970	Biafran (Nigerian Civil) War
1970s–1980s	Series of failed civilian governments and military coups in Nigeria
1974	Oil boom in Nigeria
1975	Capital of Nigeria transferred from Lagos to Abuja
1993	In Nigeria, transition from military rule to democratic rule ends when General Sanni Abacha declares himself ruler
1995	Nigeria suspended from Commonwealth after execution of nine political dissidents

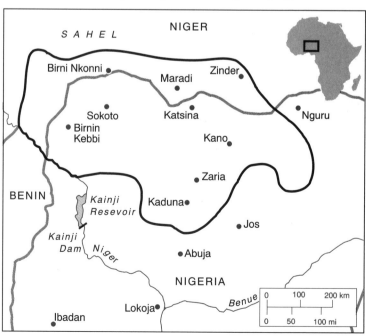

Hausa rulers. For centuries, the Fulani settlers had coexisted peacefully with the Hausa. Toward the end of the eighteenth century, however, heavy taxes imposed by the Hausa triggered a rebellion that turned into a jihad. It was supported by the rural Hausa, who also suffered under the taxation system. After a four-year struggle, all the Hausa states were conquered, and Fodio established the Fulani-Hausa Sokoto Caliphate. It continued to expand it until the caliphate reached its greatest extent in 1830. The borders of the Sokoto Caliphate remained basically the same until the British conquered the caliphate in 1903. Even today, the ruling class of Hausaland is largely made up of Fulanis.

Language

The Hausa speak a language also called Hausa, an Afroasiatic language related to Arabic, Berber, and Hebrew. It is one of the most widely spoken languages in Africa because, in the past, Hausa influence spread far beyond Hausaland thanks to trade. Hausa has been heavily influenced by Arabic. The Hausa script is called Ajemic and uses Arabic characters; the British introduced the Roman script, however, which is now more widely used. Historically, the Hausa script was used for business and government records.

Ways of life

Most Hausa work on the land, so the pattern of Hausa life is greatly influenced by the changing seasons. The climate in northern Nigeria is an extreme one, with a long, dry season from October to the end of April. This is the main period of harvest. It is also the busiest trading time as most farmers sell at least some of their produce at the local market. The markets vary from weekly to daily events depending on the size of the town or city. Kano, for instance, has a busy market every day.

Masallaci Jumaa
The Masallaci Jumaa (Friday Mosque) in Zaria was built in the nineteenth century. It was designed by the Hausa architect Babban Gwani Mikaila for Emir Abdulkarim. This *mosque* (Muslim house of worship) is a complex of buildings including a central hall of worship, entrance lobbies, and washing chambers surrounded by an external wall.

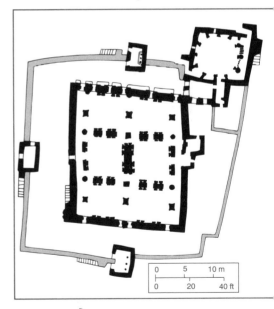

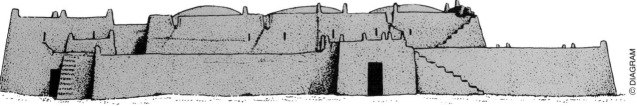

© DIAGRAM

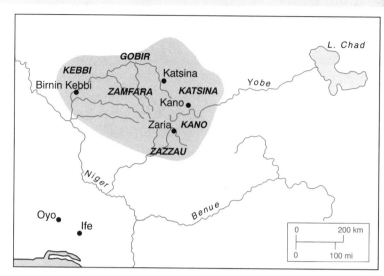

Hausa states
This map shows the regions controlled by the Hausa city-states in the seventeenth century. Each city was independent and self-governing.

Decorated wall
For centuries Hausa craftsmen have decorated houses inside with painted and molded designs, but more recently they have been applying the same techniques to the exteriors. Here is the external wall of a house in Zaria, Nigeria, decorated with modern motifs: a bicycle and a car.

Leather bag
The Hausa are famous for their artistry and skill in leatherworking. Items made include saddles and bags. This Hausa-crafted leather bag has been decorated with both *appliqué* and stitching.

From February, the weather is hot, dry, and windy. In April and May, a series of violent storms herald the arrival of the rainy season. It is during the rainy season and the months immediately before and after it that the Hausa carry out most work on the land. Cash crops grown include cotton, tobacco, and *groundnuts,* which are exported and used to make oil and peanut butter. Main food crops include rice, cereals such as millet, sorghum, and corn, and vegetables such as onions, okra, and tomatoes. The richer Hausa own cattle, often looked after by paid herders, and most also keep goats and poultry.

Agricultural work is often carried out within a cooperative system whose basic unit is the *gandu*. The sons of a family work on the gandu lands of their father in return for seed and equipment. Each son is allocated his own land to work in his own time. The produce grown on it can be used as they wish.

Although the majority of Hausa people are primarily agricultural, many have other skills apart from farming. Hausa women do little farming – they only involve themselves in harvesting. Instead, they are more involved in trading; at the market they trade in goods such as medicines, vegetable oils, and cigarettes. Hausa women also weave cloth and make goods for sale such as candy and other foods and cotton blankets, and raise goats and poultry for sale. Hausa men are weavers, dyers, blacksmiths, butchers, leatherworkers, metalworkers, barbers, or tailors as well as farmers; many are also in the Nigerian army.

Markets have their own systems of control. Each market has a headman who is responsible to the village or town leader. He has a number of assistants – often women – who are each concerned with a particular activity, for instance grain-selling or butchery. These assistants not only help the headman but also represent the interests of their own group of traders. In this way, disputes are settled and advice or help is given accordingly.

Social structure

POLITICAL STRUCTURE An *emir* (Islamic ruler) governs each Hausa state, with a group of his appointed officals who are responsible for collecting taxes and general administration. Unlike the rest of Nigeria, the northern Hausa states follow *Sharia* (Islamic holy) law.

Culture and religion

Although most Hausa people are rural and live in villages, Hausa society centers on a number of important urban areas – for example, Kano, famous for dyeing fabrics; Katsina, a trading center; and Zaria, once a major provider of slaves. In former centuries, the cities formed self-governing states, often hostile to each other but continuing to trade. The Hausa have always had trade links with Arab and Sudanese merchants, who travel across the great Sahara Desert.
RELIGION Islam was introduced to Hausaland in the 1400s, and now the majority of Hausa people are Muslim.

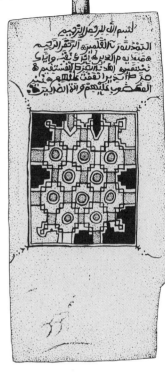

Koranic board
This wooden board from Hausaland is inscribed with a text from the Islamic holy book, the *Koran*. Such boards are used in Islamic schools for the teaching of Arabic and learning the Koran.

© DIAGRAM

Calabash bowl
Calabashes are a type of gourd. When grown, they are dried, hollowed out, and used as vessels to store foods and drinks. This calabash has been cut in two to symbolize Heaven (top half) and Earth (bottom half). The patterns have been burnt on using a hot point.

Igbo

Most Igbo live in the forested southeast of Nigeria, to the north of the *mangrove forests* of the Niger Delta. There up to thirty million Igbo divided into five main groups that differ to varying extents from each other in terms of customs, work, and religion.

History

The Igbo's origins are unknown, but it is believed that they have lived in their present location since at least the ninth century, when the Igbo Ukwu Culture flourished in the southeastern region of modern Nigeria.

In the mid-fifteenth century, Portuguese traders became the first Europeans to visit the region, and in the seventeenth, eighteenth, and nineteenth centuries, tens of thousands of Igbo were captured or bought by Dutch and British traders and sent to the Caribbean and Brazil, where they were sold as slaves. Although the slave trade was made illegal in 1807 by the British, it continued profitably for another fifty years. As the nineteenth century progressed, British traders turned their attention to exploiting the region's raw materials, in particular palm oil, timber, and ivory, relying on local intermediaries to deliver goods to them at the coast. Control of Igbo territory was difficult due to village self-rule, the fact that

Igbo timeline	
c. 800s	Igbo Ukwu Culture in existence
1400– 1500	Igbo dominated by historic Kingdom of Benin
1470	Portuguese reach Niger Delta
1807	British abolish the slave trade. Igbo involved in palm oil trade
1897	British conquer Igbo
1900	Igbo lands incorporated into British *protectorate* (colony) of Southern Nigeria
1929– 1930	Igbo Women's War against British colonial rule
1950s	Discovery of petroleum desposits in Nigeria
1960	Nigeria wins independence
1966	Igbo-led military coup staged
1967– 1970	Igbo attempt to secede from Nigeria; Biafran (Nigerian Civil) War follows
1970s– 1980s	Series of failed civilian governments and military coups in Nigeria
1974	Oil boom in Nigeria
1975	Capital of Nigeria transferred from Lagos to Abuja
1993	In Nigeria, transition from military rule to democratic rule ends when General Sanni Abacha declares himself ruler
1995	Nigeria suspended from Commonwealth after execution of nine political dissidents

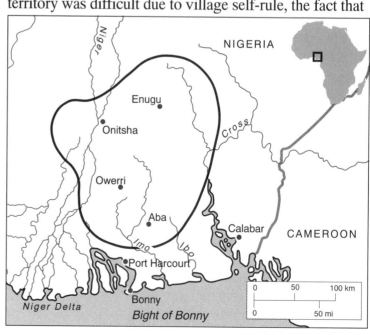

every grown man had a say in local affairs, and an absence of regional chiefs to make agreements with. Resistance to British rule was fierce, and attacks on traders and soldiers were common.

In 1900, Igbo territory became part of the British *protectorate* (colony) of Southern Nigeria which, in 1960, formed part of independent Nigeria. After independence, regional rivalries mounted, with Nigeria's political parties representing different ethnic groups. In 1966, an Igbo-led military coup was staged, and many Nigerians resented the large number of Igbo civil servants and army officers who were stationed across the country. In 1967, following riots and the slaughter of thousands of Igbo in the north and west of Nigeria, an independent Igbo state calling itself Biafra, with its capital at Enugu, was declared. The Nigerian government responded by sending the army to put down the rebels, who controlled the country's important oil reserves. Food supplies ran short, resulting in starvation and Biafran surrender in 1970. The states that form Igbo territory are now incorporated into Nigeria's federal system of government.

Language
The Igbo groups all speak dialects of Igbo, a Kwa language.

Ways of life
FARMING The Igbo village economy is based on agriculture. Due to the density of population, land is fully used. The soil is not very fertile and only a small range of crops are cultivated, including yams and cassava, plus corn and some vegetables and fruit. Igbo men are responsible for growing yams. Women have separate plots where they grow cassava and other crops. In addition to farming their own crops, Igbo women have always played other important economic roles. Women are

Metalwork
Excavations at Igbo Ukwu discovered these ninth-century bronze items – a circular altar stand (*top*) with male and female figures on opposite sides and open panels featuring snakes and spiders, and a shell-shaped container (*bottom*), possibly a wine bowl. Metal tools were made for local use or to trade with people on the coast. The Igbo are renowned for their skills in bronze casting and forging, and for the beauty of their work.

Biafran soldier
This Igbo man is a Biafran soldier. Many thousands of Igbo suffered injury and loss when Biafra tried to secede from Nigeria in 1967. The Biafran (Nigerian Civil) War ended unsuccessfully in 1970 after government troops harshly suppressed the rebellion.

© DIAGRAM

Altarpiece *(right)*
Pottery altarpieces, such as this one representing a man with his wives and attendants, were used as part of worship for *Ifijoku*, the giver and protector of yams. Yam shrines are dedicated to the Earth goddess *Ala*, and the Igbo's most important festival, the Yam Festival, is celebrated in her honor. Yams – a form of sweet potato – play a central role in the village economy.

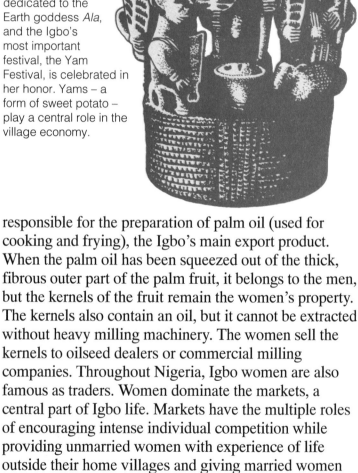

Masks
Igbo masks often represent individual spirits such as those linked with aggression and ugliness (the elephant spirit) *(below)* or beauty and peacefulness (the maiden spirit) *(above)*. Masks are of different sizes, with a community's elders wearing the larger ones to represent powerful spirits, and younger dancers wearing smaller masks for lesser spirits.

responsible for the preparation of palm oil (used for cooking and frying), the Igbo's main export product. When the palm oil has been squeezed out of the thick, fibrous outer part of the palm fruit, it belongs to the men, but the kernels of the fruit remain the women's property. The kernels also contain an oil, but it cannot be extracted without heavy milling machinery. The women sell the kernels to oilseed dealers or commercial milling companies. Throughout Nigeria, Igbo women are also famous as traders. Women dominate the markets, a central part of Igbo life. Markets have the multiple roles of encouraging intense individual competition while providing unmarried women with experience of life outside their home villages and giving married women opportunities to socialize with friends.

Social structure

Historically, the Igbo lived in small village settlements, mainly without chiefs. Igbo society is notable for encouraging individual distinction, rewarded by an increase in social standing. Except in the extreme north and west of Igbo territory where hereditary chiefs govern, rulers of communities owe their positions to age, wealth, and personal achievements.

MEN AND WOMEN Igbo women usually marry outside their villages and normally do not own land. Male children are allotted a portion of their father's land and inherit a share when he dies. This gives men economic and political power within their communities. However, the women run their own affairs by means of their own businesses and political organizations separate from the men's.

In 1929, Igbo women began demonstrating against the British colonial government. They were angry because the British were imposing a male dominated system of control on them, assuming that Igbo women held the same status as their European counterparts – dependent economically and politically on men. This meant that much of the women's state of economic and political independence was being eroded. The demonstrations became more violent as the British ignored their demands, rioting began, and finally open war broke out – the Women's War (1929–30). Since colonial times, the role of women in Igbo society has changed, but Igbo women are still recognized as being economically powerful and are often militant.

Culture and religion

RELIGION Protestant and Catholic missionaries first entered Igbo territory in the mid-nineteenth century, building churches and establishing schools. Many Igbo have since converted to Christianity, but the Igbo religion is still flourishing. It is based on reverence for *Ala* generally the Earth goddess, and a number of lesser male and female deities. Some Igbo groups also acknowledge a supreme being, *Chukwu* the creator of the Universe.

ART The Igbo are especially noted for the diversity of their sculptures. These sculptures are made of many different materials, including bronze, ivory, stone, and wood. Styles vary greatly, a reflection of the Igbo tradition of village autonomy. A variety of elaborate wooden masks are produced and used during initiations, births, weddings, burial rituals, and other celebrations.

Ancestor reverance
The Igbo people honor and remember their ancestors, who are represented at important rituals by dancers wearing masks, as above.

© DIAGRAM

West African animal fables and proverbs

Some of the most popular and most enduring West African storytelling involves animal fables, tales in which familiar animals take on human characteristics – similar to Aesop's "Fables" and Rudyard Kipling's "Just So Stories," which probably borrow from West African traditions. These animal fables – explaining how the goat became domesticated, for instance, or describing the cunning of a trickster animal – have been passed down through the ages, and have even made their way to other parts of the world. The West Africans who were taken as slaves to the Americas from the 1500s to the 1800s took with them many aspects of their culture, including dance, music, and storytelling. Many stories originated elsewhere, such as India or Europe, and were brought to Africa by migrants thousands of years ago.

Elephants
This rock painting from Tassili-n-Ajjer in the Sahara Desert depicts an elephant. In folklore an elephant can symbolize a chief, and it appears in the proverb "If you follow an elephant you don't lose your way," which means that you will be protected if you stay close to an important person.

Anansi the spider

Anansi the spider appears in a number of folk tales, in West Africa and the Caribbean, where he is often described as conceited or lazy. Usually Anansi is shown as clever, but in other stories he is outwitted. A tale explaining why spiders hide in the corners of houses describes a feud between rich Anansi and poor Chameleon: Anansi tries to steal Chameleon's field but is fooled by the cleverer animal. Anansi is left with nothing and hides in shame.

Griots
In West Africa, professional storytellers are called *griots*, and they are highly respected in many cultures. This griot to a royal court was sketched by one of the first visiting Europeans many years ago.

How Leopard got his spots
These ancient leopards from Nigeria are carved in ivory and have copper spots. The leopard features in many folk tales, usually as a fearsome animal widely admired for its strength and speed. In a Sierra Leonean fable explaining how the leopard got its spots, however, the animal is a figure of pity. The story explains that Leopard regularly visited his friend Fire and often asked Fire to visit his home. But when Fire finally visited, Leopard's house was destroyed, and Leopard and his wife were scorched by the flames, resulting in the blackened spots that all leopards have today.

Fables are intended to teach. Some fables explain a natural phenomenon: why the leopard has its spots, for instance. Others illustrate an aspect of human nature or behavior – but manifested by an animal. Trickery and cleverness are among the most common behaviors that appear. Sometimes, a fable contains a moral that is meant as a lesson to humans. Good deeds are rewarded; deceit is always punished; and wit wins over physical strength.

Tortoise and Hare
A hare climbs up the back of this Yoruba mask. Sometimes Hare is a clever character who wins by his wits. But better known is the story of the race between Hare and Tortoise. Hare, obviously faster, challenges the Tortoise to a race. But Tortoise is clever and manages to outwit Hare every time.

Uncle Remus

Many ancient folk tales were transported to the Americas by African slaves. Uncle Remus – a character created by writer Joel Chandler Harris in the late nineteenth century – is a former slave who tells stories to entertain the son of the owner of the plantation where he lives. The stories are versions of fables told by his African ancestors; they feature animal characters such as Brer Rabbit, Brer Fox, and Brer Wolf, tricksters who usually win in the end through cleverness. Rabbits, foxes and wolves aren't found in sub-Saharan Africa; the original fables probably featured spiders, hares, and hyenas.

"Tar Baby" is one such story transferred from West Africa to the American South. The Hausa tell a story called "Rubber Girl," in which Spider steals a neighbor's nuts to cover up for his not having planted any. The neighbor makes a figure of a girl out of sticky rubber resin, and when Spider sees the figure, he tries to touch it. He ends up being stuck fast to the Rubber Girl, and the neighbor beats Spider before letting him go.

Animal proverbs

Many West African proverbs featuring animals were sometimes associated with the brass gold-weights (shown below) made by the Asante people. Antelopes, crocodiles, fish, and scorpions are just a few of the animal forms used in these weights. An antelope with long horns suggests the proverb "Had I known that, but it has passed behind me," meaning have no regrets when something's done, somewhat similar to "Don't cry over spilled milk."

Continuing traditions

Many West African writers today incorporate folklore into contemporary themes. Among them are: Duro Lapido, a Nigerian playwright who has composed Yoruba folk operas; Camara Laye, a novelist from a Malinke family in Guinea, who sometimes adopted the style of a griot, or storyteller; Onuora Nzekwu, a Nigerian novelist whose work reflects the influence of Igbo folklore; and Wole Soyinka, a Nigerian poet and playwright who uses some of the themes found in Nigerian folklore in his work.

© DIAGRAM

77

Mende

Most Mende live in central and southeast Sierra Leone and they are that nation's largest single ethnic group. A few also live in western Liberia. There are presently more than one million Mende people.

History

During the thirteenth and fourteenth centuries, the ancestors of the Mende lived around the upper stretches of the Niger and Senegal rivers, in what is now Guinea. These lands formed part of the medieval Empire of Mali. Mali was declining in the fifteenth century when the Mende probably moved slowly south as part of a wave of Mande-speaking migrants that spread across West Africa.

According to Mende oral history, in the beginning of the sixteenth century a group of Manding (another Mande language) speakers called the Mani were exiled from the Empire of Mali. Under their queen, Mansarico, they traveled southwest, finally settling in the Cape Mount area of modern Liberia around 1540. From there, the Mani conquered much of present-day Sierra Leone, establishing many subkingdoms. The resulting peoples of mixed Mani and local descent formed new ethnic groups, the largest of which was the Mende.

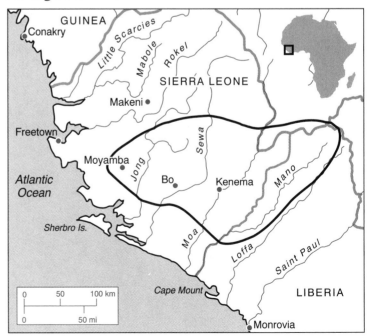

Mende timeline

1235– c. 1500	Empire of Mali: Mende ancestors part of empire
1400s	Mende begin moving southwest into present-day Sierra Leone and Liberia, conquering local peoples
c. 1500	Mani people exiled from Mali
c. 1540	Mende ancestors settled in Cape Mount area (Liberia)
1800s	Christianity spreads in Sierra Leone
1808	British rule established in Freetown (Sierra Leone)
1847	Liberia established by freed American slaves
1896	A British *protectorate* (colony) declared over Sierra Leone.
1898	Mende revolt sparked by the "hut tax"; revolt suppressed
1961	Sierra Leone independent
1967– 1969	Period of military rule in Sierra Leone
1980– 1985	Period of military rule in Liberia
1989	Civil war erupts in Liberia
1990	Assassination of Liberian president Samuel Doe; civil war escalates
1991	Sierra Leonean rebels invade from Liberia; civil war breaks out
1992	Military coup in Sierre Leone
1995	Short-lived peace accord signed in Liberia
1996	Miltary leader ousted by deputy in Sierra Leone; cease-fire declared. Fighting breaks out again in Liberia

In the early eighteenth century, the Mende began migrating west of the Sewa river. They gained control of the southern half of modern Sierre Leone by the early nineteenth century. By 1896, however, they were conquered by the British. The Mende people were among the most active in the fight for independence from colonial rule. Sierre Leone became independent in 1961, with Dr Milton Margai, a Mende, as head of state.

RECENT EVENTS In the 1990s, both Sierre Leone and Liberia have been hit by civil wars. In 1991, rebels launched an attack on Sierre Leone and the country was ripped apart by fighting between government and rebel troops. The aims of the rebels were to expel foreigners from the country and to take control of the rich diamond-mining regions. The people most affected by the conflict were ordinary civilians. Many Mende suffered through loss of employment and land, and many were victims of brutality meted out by both the government and rebel troops. The fighting was ended by a cease-fire in 1996.

Liberia has been torn apart by recurring fighting between various rebel groups since 1989. Thousands have fled the country since this date and the conflict still continues today.

Language

The Mende language, also called Mende, belongs to the Mande language group.

Ways of life

FARMING The majority of the Mende people live in rural areas and make their living from the land. Rice, cassava, and yams are important food crops. The Mende also produce crops to sell, especially coffee, cocoa, ginger, kola nuts, *groundnuts* (peanuts), and cassava. Most rice is grown on upland farms by a system called *shifting cultivation*. This involves clearing patches of forests, growing crops on the cleared land for a few years, and then moving on to let the soil recover fertility. An increasing population and the growing levels of *urbanization*, however, have pushed farmers into using more intensive methods of cultivation. Since 1923, they have been encouraged to reclaim and farm swamp lands.

Mende hairstyle
This young Mende girl's hairstyle was probably fashioned for her by a friend. To style another woman's hair is considered an act of true friendship. As the intricate plaits take a long time to do, it shows that the woman wants only the best for her friend and will not be jealous of her beauty, especially if the style is flattering. For young women, neat, tightly plaited styles are considered alluring. In older women, plaits may be looser as they do not wish to spend so much time and discomfort on their hairstyles.

© DIAGRAM

Nomori
This soap-stone *nomori* figurine was probably used by a Mende farmer to protect his rice fields. It may originally have been carved to mark a grave or as part of an ancestor cult. Nomori figurines have no set form and can vary in style widely.

© DIAGRAM

MINING Diamonds have been Sierre Leone's most important export since the 1930s. Originally, diamond mining was monopolized by a government-run company. Widespread diamond smuggling and illicit mining in the 1950s forced the government to allow the licensing of independent diggers. Today, many Mende men work as diamond diggers, either independently or as part of a gang employed by a company.

Social structure

The basic economic and social unit in Mende society is the *mawe*. Simply put, this is a farming household. It comprises one or more older men and their wives; their children; wives and husbands of these children; and any grandchildren. Although the senior male is head of the household, the functioning of the mawe is controlled by the women. The senior wife organizes the farm work, which is done by both men and women. She also has her own plot of land on which she can grow cash crops. Senior wives are therefore largely responsible for the wealth and prosperity of a mawe.

"SECRET" SOCIETIES Most Mende belong to one or more *hale* ("secret" societies). These act as unifying and controlling forces in Mende society. Hale lay down various rules, sanction acceptable forms of behavior, prohibit unacceptable behavior, and generally provide cultural and social unity to the Mende. Hale are both religious and political organizations. The officials serve as contacts with spirits who affect human affairs while, in the past, chiefs depended for their authority on support from the men's hale, *Poro.* Historically, these societies were very important as the Mende were rarely under the rule of any particular nation or state.

The most important hale are the men's society Poro, and the women's society *Sande.* At puberty, almost all boys and girls join one or the other. Initiation into Poro and

Mende attire *(above)*
This man is wearing the attire of a Mende chief. The shirt has been woven from locally grown cotton and richly embroidered; thread for weaving is more likely to be imported than locally produced today.

Minsereh figure *(right)*
Carved wooden female figures such as this are used for *divination* and healing. They are called *minsereh* and some are over 3 ft (1 m) tall. Female *diviners* of the *Yassi* society (*hale*) often use them to practice the art of spiritual healing.

Mende script *(below)*
The Mende language uses the Roman alphabet today, but in the past it was written in its own script.

Sande takes place in secret. Initiates are taken to a camp in the forest where they live in seclusion for weeks. Sande and Poro mostly teach Mende ideals of manhood and womanhood, though Poro also settles disputes and regulates trading.

Other secret societies include the *Humui, Njayei,* and *Kpa.* The Humui regulates sexual behavior; the Njayei uses herbs and other substances to cure madness, which is attributed to breaching this society's taboos; and Kpa apprentices learn to use herbs to treat minor ailments.

Recently, the activities of secret socities have been drastically affected by foreign ideas and by changes in Sierre Leonean society. Many of the rites are no longer performed in larger urban areas. In such areas, it would be impossible to ensure that everyone in the vicinity followed the necessary prohibitions on behavior while the events took place; people no longer observe *taboos* as they once did. In cities, initiation into Poro now involves simply paying the society's membership fees. Sande no longer *circumcises* girls and has incorporated prenatal and postnatal education, as well as medical developments into its initiates' lessons. Newly initiated girls return smartly dressed in modern adult clothes.

Culture and religion

RELIGION The majority of the Mende profess either Christianity or Islam. The Mende religion is still widely followed, even by converts to these world religions. The Mende religion involves belief in a supreme god, *Ngewo,* who created everything; belief in an afterlife; various nature spirits associated with such things as forests and rivers; spirits linked to particular hale; and the reverance of ancestor spirits.

CEREMONIES AND RITUALS Masked members of the Poro and Sande societies represent spirits at ceremonies. These are held to mark events such as the coming out of a group of initiates or, in the past, to make crops grow. Dancing and singing play an important part of Sande initiations, at the climax of which a woman disguised as a spirit whips away witches and unfriendly spirits. Today, these dances are largely performed to entertain.

Sande masquerades
The major character at a Sande *masquerade* is *Sowo* – the spirit of Sande. Only a senior Sande official who is an expert dancer wears the wooden mask and raffia-covered cloth costume of Sowo. *Sowo-wui* are the wooden heads that complete Sowo costumes. Each sowo-wui is unique. The Mende do not view these masks as separate entities. They have to be lightweight and are worn on top of the head like helmets. They depict the Mende ideal of feminine beauty, with delicate features, high foreheads, and elaborate coiffures. Rolls at the base of the mask represent a ringed neck – the height of beauty. The mask is stained a deep black color, as the Mende prize very black skin. Palm oil rubbed into the wood makes it resemble glossy skin.

© DIAGRAM

81

African colonists in Sierra Leone and Liberia

The slave trade indirectly led to the establishment of new communities on the West African coast: Freetown, now the capital of Sierra Leone, and Monrovia, now the capital of Liberia. Both were peopled by former slaves and their descendants who had been forcibly transported from their homes in West Africa to Britain and the Americas. They were established by abolitionists in Britain and the United States (US), both as a way to atone for the horrors of the slave trade and to resolve what was a growing social problem regarding the undefined role of former slaves.

Freetown: a community of "recaptives"

Freetown was established in the late eighteenth century by an English humanitarian group, the Sierra Leone Company. It was settled by freed slaves from Britain (some of the men accompanied by their white English wives), who were joined by freed slaves from Nova Scotia, including Maroons – former slaves from Jamaica who had been deported to Nova Scotia after an initially successful revolt against their owners – and by former slaves who had

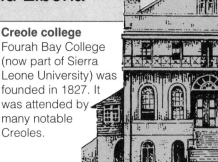

Creole college
Fourah Bay College (now part of Sierra Leone University) was founded in 1827. It was attended by many notable Creoles.

sided with the British in the American War of Independence in exchange for their freedom.

The new settlers of Freetown were not well received by the African population. The local Temne people would not give up land to the colonists, and in 1789 the Temne nearly destroyed Freetown. In 1807 Sierra Leone was made a British colony, and the population increased with more people freed from slave ships by British antislavery activists.

Most of these settlers – also called "recaptives" and the descendants of whom are today called "Creoles" – were converted to Christianity and educated in English traditions. But many, especially those who were Yoruba, also retained their African culture and language, resulting in the mix of English and African languages that are known as Creole languages. Some also returned to their homelands: Samuel Ajayi Crowther, a Yoruba Creole and the first black bishop of the Anglican Church, returned to his native Nigeria and became a well-known historian and writer on the Yoruba language.

In the late nineteenth century, the Creoles – who had become the educated elite of Sierra Leone – were replaced in positions of power by white Europeans. Nevertheless, they continued to have a major influence on the development of the country, and in particular on the rise of African nationalism. They were at the forefront of the independence movement that began in the 1930s.

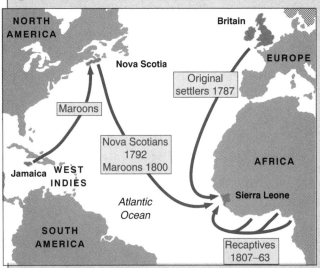

Paths to Sierra Leone
Freed slaves came from Jamaica, via Nova Scotia, and from Britain to settle Freetown in the eighteenth century.

Monrovia: "asylum from degradation"

Monrovia was founded in 1847 by a white philanthropic group called the American Colonization Society, though settlers had already been arriving in the region since the 1820s. Named after James Monroe, US president at the time, it was a settlement for freed slaves from the US. The Americans were also joined by thousands of Africans who were freed by US patrol vessels trying to interrupt the slave trade. These liberated slaves – the "Congoes," as they came to be called – were soon absorbed into what became the Americo-Liberian community.

The attitude of the newcomers toward the region's inhabitants differed little from that of white settlers toward Africans in other parts of the continent. The Americo-Liberians were determined to retain American culture and so-called "civilized" standards and resisted integration with the "tribals" – the name they gave to the indigenous population.

The Americo-Liberians and their descendants were always a minority but, until the 1980s, they were Liberia's elite, providing most of the country's presidents. Also, the professions of law and the senior ranks of the civil service were dominated by Americo-Liberians, who shunned agriculture, seeing it as a reminder of their slave origins.

Americo-Liberians were devout Christians – most were members of the long-established American Episcopal, Baptist, or Methodist churches – and placed great importance in symbols of Western culture so as to distance themselves from what they saw as "barbarous" Africa. They built houses in the style of the American South and dressed in formal European clothing (including top hats and tailcoats on state occasions), which was inappropriate in the tropics. Their children were usually sent abroad to complete their studies, often to the US.

President's residence
The style of the American South was visible in Americo-Liberian architecture, such as the president's official residence

It was common practice for Americo-Liberians to bring African children into their homes, raise them as Christians, and teach them English. Following the custom of white Southern US plantation owners, Americo-Liberian men often kept "tribal" wives in addition to having a wife from their own social background. Children of such unions were often adopted by the Americo-Liberian family, contributing to the gradual merging of Americo-Liberians with indigenous peoples that exists today.

Declaration of Independence (*excerpts below*)
Liberia's Declaration of Independence written in 1847 when the Republic of Liberia was established, explains why Americans settled in Africa and expresses the aspirations that they had brought with them.

"We, the people of the Republic of Liberia, were originally inhabitants of the United States of North America.

In some parts of that country we were debarred from all rights and privileges of men – in other parts, public sentiment, more powerful than law, frowned us down....

We were made a separate and distinct class and against us every avenue of improvement was effectually closed. Strangers from other lands, of a color different from ours, were preferred before us....

...we looked with anxiety for some asylum from the deep degradation....

...In coming to the barbarous shores of Africa we indulged the pleasing hope that we would be permitted to exercise and improve those faculties which impart to man his dignity...."

Moors

The name "Moor" has been applied to many different peoples over the centuries. For years it was used to describe the people of Morocco and also the Muslims from North Africa who conquered large parts of Spain in the Middle Ages. Today, it generally refers to the people who make up seventy percent of the population of Mauritania. It also applies to a few of the people of Western Sahara, which has been occupied by Morocco – and, for a while, Mauritania – since 1975.

There are probably about 1,500,000 Moors. There are two main Moor groups: the Bidanis, or "White Moors," who are of Berber-Arab origin; and the Sudanis, or "Black Moors," who are largely of Black African origin and are related to the Fulani, Soninke, Tukolor, Wolof, and other peoples.

History

The original ancestors of today's Moors are said to have moved into what is now Mauritania in the eleventh century, with the spread of the Berber Almoravids led by Abu Bakr. Others followed in subsequent centuries.

The Moors fall into several subgroups. Two of the most important are the Hassani and Zawiya, both Bidani. The

Moors timeline

c. 1070	Moors arrive in West Africa with invading Almoravids
c. 1400s	Trade with Europeans begins
1644–1674	Cherr Baba War; Hassani and Zawiya Moors emerge
1700s–1800s	Moors involved in flourishing gum arabic trade
1903	Mauritania becomes a French colony
1959	Moktar Ould Daddah elected prime minister of Mauritania
1960	Maurtianian independence
1960s	Discovery of iron ore and copper deposits in Mauritania
1960s–1980s	Recurring *droughts* cause famine in Sahelian countries
1964	Mauritania declared a one-party state
1966	Arabicization campaign; violence erupts between Moors and other peoples
1974	Mainly foreign-controlled iron mines are nationalized
1976	Mauritania and Morocco invade Western Sahara
1978	Ould Daddah overthrown
1979	Mauritania renounces claim to Western Sahara
1980	Civilian government formed. Slavery abolished
1984	Lieutenant Colonel Ould Taya takes power in military coup
1990s	Islamicization policy favored instead of Arabicization – to ease ethnic tension
1992	Ould Taya elected President
1994	Government cracks down on radical Islamic groups

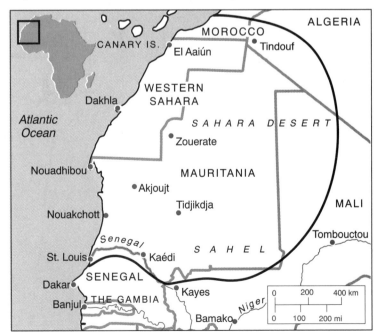

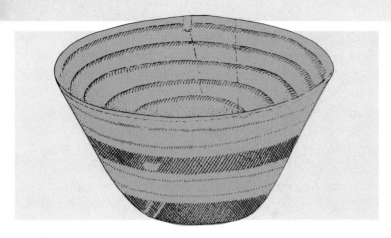

Wooden bowl
The Moors use wood for many items, including dishes. This type of bowl is used for heating milk. Hot stones are placed inside, with the milk, and the taste of burning milk is thought to keep away evil spirits.

Clothing
A man typically wears a long robe, with baggy trousers and a shirt underneath, and covers his head with a turban. In cold weather, he may add a cloak made of wool or sheepskin. A woman typically wears baggy trousers and a long tunic, with a shawl to cover her head when needed. Moorish women rarely veil their faces. Blue is a popular color for the clothing of both sexes.

Hassani descend from a group of Arab people who settled in Mauritania from the fifteenth century onward. Moorish history holds that the division into Hassani and Zawiya occurred as a result of the Cherr Baba War between the Berbers and the Arabs in 1644–74.

RECENT CONFLICTS There have long been rivalries between the majority Moor population and the minority Black African population of Mauritania. Since the 1980s, this animosity has often turned into open conflict; there have been many instances of violence. The government troops' support of the Moors in these conflicts has led to the death of hundreds of Black African Mauritanians.

Language

The language of almost all the Moors is Arabic. French is also widely spoken in Mauritania – a relic of colonial days. A few Moors speak Berber languages.

Ways of life

About sixty percent of Moors live in rural areas, and the rest in towns. Industrialization and *urbanization* are attracting many people away from their *nomadic* ways of life, in which they travel over a large area with their herds of animals in search of water and pasture. Many people now work in the copper and iron mines concentrated in the northwest of the country. Young Moors from all ranks study at the University of Nouakchott, Mauritania's capital, or at other universities in Africa or abroad.

NOMADISM Most of Mauritania is desert, unsuitable for agriculture. For this reason, many Moors are nomads.

© DIAGRAM

Cattle are the mainstay of the nomads, but they also keep flocks of sheep and goats, besides camels, donkeys, and horses. Most of the cattle are in the southern part of the country, where the Sahara Desert gives way to the semidesert region of the Sahel. During the wet season, the cattle herders roam the Sahel, moving to pastures along the banks of the Senegal River during the dry season. Camels, goats, and sheep are herded in the desert.

FARMING Settled farmers live in the southern region, where they grow corn, dates, melons, millet, pulses, rice, sorghum, and vegetables and raise chickens. Many farmers also live in the scattered *oases* (fertile pockets in the desert), where there is enough water for agriculture.

DIVISION OF LABOR Men do most of the herding and heavy agricultural work. Women make goods from leather and weave cloth, including the fabric of tents. Among the nomads, it is the women who set up the tents and take them down again.

DROUGHT AND DESERTIFICATION During the 1960s and 1980s, *droughts* (periods of inadequate rainfall) struck Mauritania; the country was devastated and the nomadic Moors, in particular, were badly affected. Cropping on the flood plains of the Senegal River was impossible because it failed to flood; over a million cattle were lost; and death rates for vulnerable people rose. Refugees flocked to urban areas in search of emergency food supplies, putting great strain on the resources of these areas.

Over the years, patches of the fragile Sahelian lands have been turning into desert, threatening the farming and grazing lands of the Moors. This process of *desertification* has been worsened by drought and also threatens the ability of rural people to make a living from the land. Drought and desertification have caused not only great immediate distress but also disrupted the nomadic pattern so severely that many will probably not return to that lifestyle. For example, in 1963, eighty-three percent of the population was nomadic, but by 1980 this figure was only twenty-five percent. Drought and desertification have also caused the remaining nomadic Moors to alter their habits. For instance, they may stay in

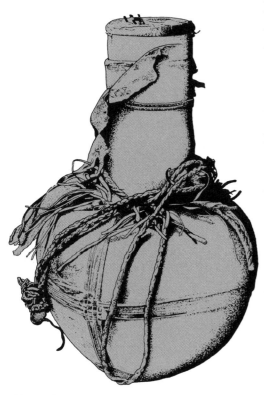

Butter jar
This jar, made of leather and rope, would have been used by Moorish nomads to carry butter. Butter is an important food item, but is also used as a cosmetic.

one place for longer if they know there is a water supply available. This has put many cattle herders into conflict with the settled farming populations. In fact, in recent decades there have been many instances of violent conflict between the Moor and non-Moor populations.

Social structure

There are many *clans* (groups of several extended families who share a common ancestor or ancestors) within the subgroups and a strong class structure exists. The highest class is that of the nobles. Some subgroups serve the nobles, and slavery was not abolished in Mauritania until 1980. Below the nobles come smiths, wandering entertainers, and the *imraguen*, or fishermen, on the coast. Each subgroup has its own code of laws and has civilian and religious leaders who inherit their positions from their fathers. Some Moors are *marabouts*, or holy men. A few families are considered particularly holy because they are claim descent from of the Prophet Muhammad. In the past, the Bidanis were considered superior to the Sudanis, though a Sudani of noble birth could outrank an ordinary Bidani – the division was based on class not color.

MARRIAGE People tend to marry within their clans. One man may have several wives, but men generally only marry a new wife after divorcing the previous one, rarely keeping more than one or two wives at a time.

Culture and religion

RELIGION The vast majority of Moors are Muslim.

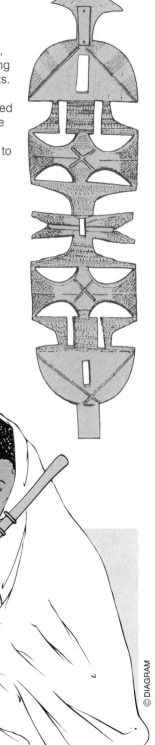

Wooden pole
Carved wooden poles are used to hang leather bags, dishes, and cooking utensils inside tents. The bottom of the poles are sharpened so that they can be pushed into the ground and made to stand upright.

Gourd harp
These stringed musical instruments are made from gourds. The design is very old, similar ones were used in Ancient Egypt. Historically, the dominant Moor groups retained musicians to sing their praises and entertain them.

© DIAGRAM

87

Mossi

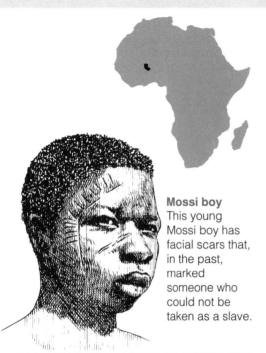

Mossi boy
This young Mossi boy has facial scars that, in the past, marked someone who could not be taken as a slave.

M ossi as a term refers to a number of different ethnic groups who have similar cultures and lifestyles but maintain some distinct ethnic identity. The Yarse, for instance, are one group within Mossi society. Together, the groups that make up Mossi society represent half the population of Burkina Faso.

There are about four million Mossi. Most live in Burkina Faso, but some 500,000 Mossi have emigrated to live and work in cities or on plantations in Ghana, Ivory Coast, and France.

History

Mossi oral history states that Mossi society originated in the fifteenth century when a cavalry group from northern Ghana rode north in search of land. The invaders conquered the various farming peoples who inhabited the valley of the White Volta River and settled among them. Some of the peoples in the area fled to locations where the invaders' horses could not follow, such as to Mali's isolated Bandiagara Cliffs where the Dogon people sought refuge. Other peoples, however, remained behind in the newly created kingdoms, which included Ouagadougou, Ouahigouya (or Yatenga), Dagomba, and Namumba and became part of a new society known as the Mossi.

Mossi timeline

late 1400s	White Volta area invaded by horsemen from Ghana; Mossi society founded. Ouagadougou Kingdom founded by Naba Oubri
mid-1500s	Ouahigouya (or Yatenga) kingdom founded by Naba Yadega
1591	Mossi defeated by Moroccan invaders
1744–1745	Asante Empire occupies Dagomba, a Mossi kingdom
1897	France takes control of Ouagadougou
1919	Upper Volta declared a separate colonial territory under France
1960	Independence from French rule
1969–1974	Prolonged *drought* causes crisis among Burkina Faso farmers, including Mossi
1984	Upper Volta renamed Burkina Faso

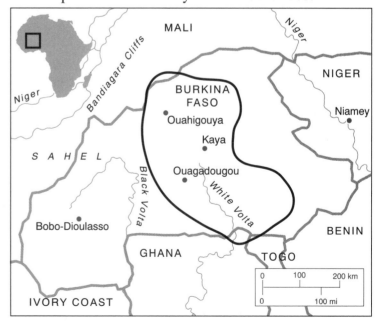

The conquerors became the ruling class and were called the *nakomsé* ("the right and power to rule"). The defeated farmers became the commoners and were called *nyonyosé* – "the ancient ones" or "children of the earth," references to their origins as the original inhabitants of Mossi territory. The nakomsé generally respected the nyonyosé, maintaining preexisting *clans* (several extended families who share a common ancestor or ancestors) and assimilating many of their traditions into the new society. This reduced the likelihood of revolt and explains the cultural variations that are still found in Mossi society. Today, there continues to be a distinction between nakomsé and nyonyosé in terms of power relationships, but these have been lessened by intermarriage.

COLONIALISM In 1897, France gained control of Mossi territory: Mossi myth explains that they were conquered not because they were weaker than the French, but because the ruler of Ouagadougou had ignored the warnings of the gods. French direct influence over the Mossi remained limited, however, because the conquerors did not consider the area to be economically important. France's administrative hold over the Mossi remained weak, and it was subject to frequent revolts over such issues as the imposition of taxes, forced labor, and military conscription. When Burkina Faso (then known as Upper Volta) gained its independence from France in 1960, its first president, Maurice Yameogo, was a Mossi.

Doll (right)
Dolls are produced in different shapes and sizes and represent different Mossi *clans* or regions. Sometimes they are used as fertility symbols – they may be carried on the back by a woman having problems conceiving. More often, dolls are used as children's toys for use in role play, as in many other cultures.

Shelter post (left)
Forked support posts like the one shown held up shelters that provided shade for community meetings, which were presided over by Mossi chiefs. Few decorated posts – this one shows a figure of a woman – are in use today.

Mogho naba
A *mogho naba* (center) surrounded by his chiefs (naba). The mogho naba was the supreme ruler of the Mossi, and the role is still important today, though less powerful than in the past. He rules from the court of Ouagadougou, now the capital of Burkina Faso.

© DIAGRAM

Diviner

A Mossi *diviner* seeks guidance in sand patterns. As in other cultures, the diviner is a sort of oracle, interpreting messages concerning major life decisions using various *divination* methods.

Language

The Mossi language, called Moré (or Moore or Molé), is one of the Niger-Congo family of languages.

Ways of life

In the seventeenth and eighteenth centuries, large towns and markets developed through which goods such as salt and dried fish were imported and cotton cloth, livestock, and surplus grain exported. This led to specializations within Mossi society and the creation of specialized occupational groups such as blacksmiths and weavers. These were once associated with separate ethnic groups; the Yarse, for example, were largely weavers and traders. But these distinctions were flexible, so that a person could change from one group to another throughout a lifetime.

Most Mossi, however, live in rual areas and are subsistence farmers, producing cereals, yams, and legumes, and providing for themselves off the land. Poor soil and an increasing population, however, have made it more difficult to grow enough crops. For this reason, over the years Mossi farmers have shifted their farms, leading to a continuous shifting of the population. This has further contributed to the diversity of Mossi society.

Social structure

Mossi society is based on extended families, each of which typically consists of the head of the family, his wife, their children and grandchildren, and other close relatives. These extended families are grouped together into clans. The members of a clan have the same surname and claim descent from a common ancestor, and each clan is symbolically represented by an animal.

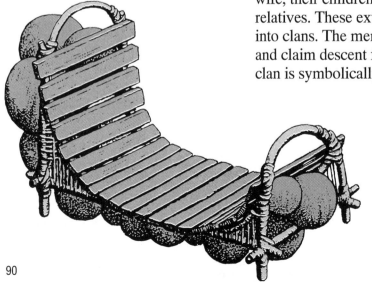

Calabash balafon

In a *balafon* – a type of xylophone common throughout Africa – the wooden keys are attached to calabashes of different sizes, providing a range of sounds. The Mossi, in common with other African peoples, use calabashes for many instruments. A technique unique to the Mossi is to fill a large calabash bowl with water, place a smaller calabash bowl, upside down, on the water, and strike the floating calabash.

Culture and religion

RELIGION Muslim traders from the north helped to introduce Islam to West Africa in the early years of the second millenium. Since this date, most have converted to Islam, nevertheless many Mossi people have remained faithful to the Mossi religion, which is based on the devotion to ancestors and spirits.

WEAVING Since the integration of weavers of Mande origin into Mossi society in c. 1600, the Mossi have been renowned for their cotton and silk weaving. Some Mossi groups tell a creation myth that recalls how the founding ancestor was a weaver who descended to earth on the threads from his loom.

Weaving is done by men during the dry season, but women usually dye the woven strips in pits filled with *indigo* (deep blue) dye. Some of the resulting blue-and-white strips are combined to form a larger cloth. Despite competition from industrial textile mills, this traditional cloth is still highly sought after and is passed down through the generations in families.

MASKS The Mossi are well known for their masks, used in celebrations. In the past, only the nyonyosé used masks, typically painted intense shades of red, white, black, and sometimes brown. Masks are owned by individual families or clans and are passed down through generations. The masks can be used to invoke protection and serve as a direct means of communication with the owners' ancestors and celebrate individual and group identity. In some regions, women and children are prohibited from viewing mask appearances, while in others both men and women, old and young, participate in performances.

Mossi masks, which are usually tall, are often carved from the soft, fine-grained, and very lightweight wood of the ceiba tree. Ceiba wood is very susceptible to insect damage, however, and every year, after the harvest but before the dry season, all the masks in a village are soaked in a river or a swamp to kill any insects and to remove the paint applied to the masks the previous year.

Masks
Mossi masks are varied in appearance. They can be over 6 ft (180 cm) high.

1 This wooden mask may represent an albino. The ridge extending from the mask's forehead is carved to resemble a rooster's comb.
2 This mask has an antelope figure as the face, and a human figure makes up the mask's superstructure, which is many times the height of the facial covering. .

1

2

Superstars of the West African music scene

Contemporary West African popular music generally involves a fusion of traditional African musical styles with American forms such as jazz, blues, and reggae – themselves styles that derive from West Africa through 500 years of contact. In recent years, West African musicians have attracted a worldwide following. Afro–Beat, juju, Ghanaian highlife and other high-energy dance music styles with their larger-than-life stars have excited tremendous interest, but so too have the sensual music and songs of the jali – the traditional caste of Malian and Guinean musical storyteller or griot.

Abidjan (Ivory Coast) Dakar (Senegal) and Lagos (Nigeria) are the main regional centers of the West African music industry. Because of sophisticated recording facilities and commercial networks, however, European cities such as Paris – and to a lesser extent London – have become major poles of attraction for West African musicians. To reach a wider international audience, many musicians use French or English lyrics.

Kora players

Master *kora* players performing *Casamance-style music*, a percussive style from the region of the same name in southern Senegal and Gambia.

Instruments

Traditional instruments are fundamentally important for West African musicians, but "Western" instruments have also been widely adopted.

DRUMS A huge variety of drums provides most of the rhythmic qualities so typical of West African music. "Talking drums," so called because they are used to mimic the tonal qualities of African languages, are just one of the many types of traditional drums used widely throughout West Africa.

Musical "greats"
Cesaria Evora (left)

Cape Verde's music is remarkable for its diversity of styles – many little altered through the centuries. Portugal left a major impact on Cape Verde's music, but mainland African, Brazilian, and Caribbean influences are also clear. Despite its beauty, Cape Verde's music is little known beyond its shores except among the emigrant communities in Portugal and Massachusetts, US. One recent exception is Paris-based Cesaria Evora whose slow-paced, nostalgic ballads sung in a Creole language are so typical of Cape Verde.

Anjeline Kidjo

Few women from West Africa have made it to superstar status. One who has is vocalist Angelique Kidjo, from Benin. She sings in Fon, and her music reflects the style of *zilin*, a Fon-region singing style similar to the blues.

King Sunny Ade (left)

Juju has been a popular music style since the 1920s, when it originated – then called palm-wine music – among the Yoruba in Lagos, but it took on a more modern form when Nigerian musician IK Dairo introduced electric guitars, the accordion, and the talking drum into juju songs. This led to the spread of juju around the globe and made Dairo an international star. In the late 1970s, King Sunny Ade, a Yoruba musician, took over the role of "juju king."

KORA *The kora usually has twenty-one to twenty-five strings and resembles a cross between a harp and a lute. The instrument probably originated in what is now Guinea-Bissau, but today the most famous kora players are from Mali, and they often play electrified versions of the instrument.*

XYLOPHONE *The xylophone is widely played, especially in Mali and Guinea. It has eighteen to twenty-one keys suspended on a bamboo frame over gourd resonators, and is often played by two people. The balafon is one type of xylophone widely used throughout West Africa.*

GUITAR *The traditional instrument of Cape Verde, the guitar became popular elsewhere in West Africa with the return of African soldiers and sailors from overseas after World War II. Standard and electric guitars are widely played, and distinct African styles have developed, such as the juju style.*

BRASS *Cuban rmusic has been popular in West Africa since before Wordl War II, its saxophones and other brass wind instruments have become important features of West African dance music.*

Drum talk

A *kalungu*, a type of talking drum from Nigeria, imitates the tone of the speech. It is hourglass-shaped, and the pitch can be adjusted by tightening the "waist."

Oding player (right)
A woman from Cameroon plays the *oding*, a traditional flute played only by women. The flute is filled with water before being played.

Salif Keita (right)
To a great extent, it is thanks to Salif Keita's fusion album *Soro* that Malian music came to international attention in the early 1980s. Keita's high-tech Paris and Los Angeles arrangements are impressive, and he has brought attention to the more traditional Malian musicians, such as the remarkable *kora* player Toumani Diabaté.

Fela Kuti
Born into an elite Yoruba family, Fela Kuti studied trumpet and musicology in London, England before returning to Nigeria in 1963. Kuti's blend of *highlife,* jazz, and Yoruba music became known as *Afro-Beat*, and he quickly rose to national stardom. His music is less easily accessible (and less dance oriented) than that of many of his compatriots. As an outspoken critic – in his lyrics and off stage – of Nigerian military regimes and the British and US governments, Kuti has been subject to harassment, house-arrest, and imprisonment in Nigeria.

Youssou N'Dour (right)
Fusing Cuban music and traditional styles from his native Senegal, Youssou N'Dour – born into a *griot* (storyteller) family – became a superstar at home before conquering the world in the 1980s. N'Dour sings mainly in Wolof, and his lyrics relate to the experiences of his original fans, the inhabitants of the poor neighborhoods of the capital city Dakar. He has recently set up a recording studio in Dakar.

Yoruba

T he Yoruba mainly live in the southwest of Nigeria, in eastern Benin, and in parts of Togo. There are approximately twelve million Yoruba.

History

Through their myths, the Yoruba believe that they have lived in their present homeland for thousands of years. The kingdom of Ife is accepted as the birthplace of the Yoruba as a separate people. The town of Ife is considered to be the Yoruba spiritual capital, perhaps having emerged in the seventh or eighth century. The Yoruba's traditional ruling families are able to trace their ancestors back to the twelfth century.

From Ife new Yoruba kingdoms were later established, the most powerful being Oyo in the grasslands to the north. Oyo grew into a great empire, controlling the trade routes linking the sea with the north. In the eighteenth century, the Oyo Empire was torn apart by civil war, collapsing completely in the 1830s. After the demise of Oyo, Ibadan became the most powerful Yoruba town, eventually controlling a large empire. European slave traders benefited from Yoruba divisions, with rival kings capturing and selling large numbers of their enemies into

Yoruba timeline

600s on	Emergence of Ife Kingdom
1300s	Bronze and terra-cotta sculpture produced in Ife. Oyo state founded
1510	Start of Atlantic slave trade
1789	Oyo Empire reaches greatest extent
1836	Oyo dominated by Sokoto Caliphate: Oyo dissolves
1862	Ibadan Empire established in Nigeria and becomes most powerful in region
1897	British conquest of Yorubaland completed
1950s	Discovery of pertroleum desposits in Nigeria
1960	Nigeria wins independence
1967– 1970	Biafran (Nigerian Civil) War between Yoruba and northern Nigerians against eastern (mainly Igbo) secessionists
1970s– 1980s	Series of failed civilian governments and military coups in Nigeria
1974	Oil boom in Nigeria
1975	Capital of Nigeria transferred from Lagos to Abuja
1993	In Nigeria, transition from military rule to democratic rule ends when General Sanni Abacha declares himself ruler
1995	Nigeria suspended from Commonwealth after execution of nine political dissidents

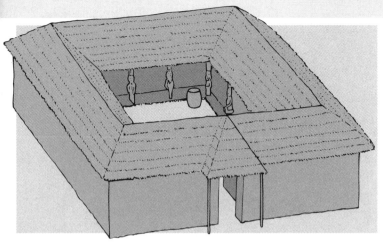

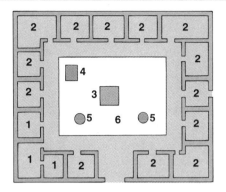

Yoruba compound
Extended families live together in *compounds,* which comprise several buildings surrounding one or more courtyards. In the past, common construction materials were mud for the thick walls, wood for beams and posts, and straw and palm leaves for the thatched roofs, which together helped to keep the buildings cool. Today, however, concrete and metal sheeting are more often used in building.

1 Rooms for the head of the compound.
2 Isolated rooms for the wives or for the family's married male children and their wives.
3 Shrine
4 Storehouse
5 Dye pit
6 Courtyard

slavery for transportation to the Americas. Even today clear elements of Yoruba culture survive in the Americas, in particular in Brazil.

COLONIALISM As the nineteenth century progressed, more and more British traders, missionaries, soldiers, and government officials entered Yoruba territory, making agreements with local kings or forcefully stripping power from those who resisted, often destroying and looting their towns. By 1897, the British had established control over the Yoruba and the region was incorporated into the *protectorate* (colony) of Southern Nigeria in 1900.

RECENT EVENTS The Yoruba played an important role in Nigeria's gaining independence in 1960; since then they have continued to be of major importance in political life.

Language
In the past, the Yoruba spoke a number of dialects of Kwa, a branch of the Niger-Congo family of languages. Over the past hundred years, however, a common version of their language has developed called Yoruba. There is a rich heritage of literature and poetry written in Yoruba; the playwright Duro Lapido is one example of a well-known writer in the Yoruba language.

Ways of life
TOWN KINGDOMS Although an agricultural people, the Yoruba have always lived in towns – Ibadan was the largest city south of the Sahara in precolonial Africa. In a typical Yoruba town the majorty are farmers and a few are artisans or traders. Farms can be up to 20 miles (8 km)

Clothing
This Yoruba woman from Nigeria ia wearing a brightly colored outfit made from a combination of locally produced cloth and imported waxed cotton.

© DIAGRAM

95

Sango staff
Yoruba religion and art are closely intertwined. During a festival, a *Sango* priest would probably rest this beautiful wooden staff on his shoulder.

Gelede dancer
Once intended to appease local witches, *gelede* dances are still held at regular intervals, but now largely to entertain. The Yoruba have many *masquerades,* which involve elaborately costumed characters such as this one.

from town and produce a wide range of crops including yams, cassava, and cocoa.

Historically, Yoruba towns were enclosed by a high wall with the palace of the *oba* (king) marking the central point. In front of the palace was the central market and around the palace were grouped the interconnecting courtyards, houses, and rooms that formed the *compounds* where other families lived. The compounds could be huge, often housing more than a thousand people. In modern times, compounds have largely been replaced by two-story houses, and many oba have built luxurious palaces.

Social structure

POLITICAL STRUCTURE The position of oba is held by a descendant of the town's founder, passing in turn to princes from several ruling houses. Decision-making powers, however, were held by a council of chiefs, made up of representatives of the town's families. Chiefs would meet every day in a palace courtyard, sending their decisions to the *oba* for formal approval. This form of government made it possible to unite the people of each town together. This system, however, meant that it was extremely difficult to unite with neighboring towns making resistance to colonial rule difficult.

Culture and religion

POLITICAL Today, over half of the Yoruba are Muslim or Christian. Even so, the Yoruba religion remains important to Yoruba life and culture, although some of the purest forms are found not in Nigeria but amongst the descendants of former Yoruba slaves living in Brazil. Yoruba religion centres on a supreme god, *Olodumare* (the owner of Heaven), but few temples or shrines are erected in his honor. This is because he is considered detached from everyday life so lesser deities are more likely to be approached to deal with specific situations. These deities or spirits can act as intermediaries between Olodumare and his followers; called *orisa*, they concern themselves with the affairs of the Earth. Each orisa has its own cult, priests, temples, and shrines. Orisa have two

Obas

In the past, much ceremony surrounded *obas* (kings), who spent most of their time hidden from view. They appeared in public only at important events and even then surrounded by attendants and totally veiled by a crown and robe made of thousands of coral beads.

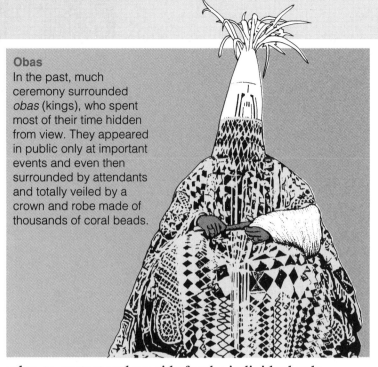

Sango shrine figure

Recognizable for the double ax-head shape at the top, carvings such as this one would appear on an altar devoted to the *orisa* (god) *Sango*. Associated with thunder, storms, and rain, Sango priests are sometimes approached to act as rainmakers.

roles, to protect and provide for the individual cult member and to provide a particular service to all members of the community. There are hundreds of orisa, some considered more important than others. *Obatala* is the most important of the orisa as the chief representative of Olodumare on Earth. Obatala was taught to create the human form into which Olodumare then put life. *Esu* is the messenger of good and evil and the main link between Heaven and Earth. Esu, often described as the "trickster god," tells Olodumare of the activities of the other orisa and of people. *Sango* is associated with thunderstorms and the anger of Olodumare. *Yemoja* is a female orisa, associated with water, rivers, lakes, and streams. *Olokun* is an orisa who lives in the sea, controlling its anger and sharing its riches. Over time, orisas can acquire new associations. For example, *Ogun,* the god associated with iron and other metals and metalwork, is often shown respect by taxi drivers, who have singled him out for to provide protection while they drive their vehicles – as cars are made from metal.

Respect for ancestors forms a major part of the Yoruba religion. Dances and dramas are performed to praise the dead and promote the well-being of the community.

Door panel *(below)*

Intricately carved with tiny figures, this door panel is in the Nigerian Museum in Lagos.

The historic Kingdom of Benin

Historic Benin was a city-state, and later a kingdom, in what is now southeastern Nigeria. (The present independent country of Benin – known as Dahomey until 1975 – lies to the west of Nigeria and has no direct connection with this Benin.) The capital of the old empire was Benin City, which still stands on a branch of the Benin River and is the capital of the modern Nigerian province of Edo (another name for Benin and its inhabitants).

The king of Benin had the title of oba. *He was an absolute monarch, but he had many religious duties and left the actual government to his ministers. The first known oba was a Yoruba prince from Ife called Oranmiyan, who became ruler in about 1176, though local dynasties existed before this date. About forty obas have held office since Oranmiyan, though the power of the current oba is limited to local government.*

Kingdom of Benin
The historic Kingdom of Benin was in what is now southeastern Nigeria.

People and trade

The Kingdom of Benin reached its greatest extent in the two hundred years beginning in the mid-1400s. It reached as far west as modern Lagos, where Benin set up a ruling dynasty. The people of Benin were the Bini, who spoke a language also called Bini. They were farmers, hunters, and warriors. Their artists made fine sculptures in metal and terra cotta. The most important works of art were made of brass, though they are often called Benin "bronzes," and include plaques, statues, busts, masks, and jewelry.

Benin became wealthy through trade with other African peoples, mostly in such goods as copper, foodstuffs, ivory, and salt. The first Europeans to visit Benin were Portuguese explorers, who reached

Queen Mother
This brass bust of a *queen mother* is thought to date from the 1500s. The title of queen mother was introduced by Oba Esigie, whose reign began about 1504. He wanted to honor his own mother.

the coast in 1485. They have left the earliest descriptions of Benin City and its people. For several years the Portuguese traded with Benin, mostly buying peppers and slaves. Benin wanted firearms, which the Portuguese refused to supply. The rulers of Benin decided not to continue to sell slaves, and trade with Europe languished for about two hundred years. In the late 1800s, the Bini resumed selling slaves to European dealers.

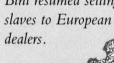

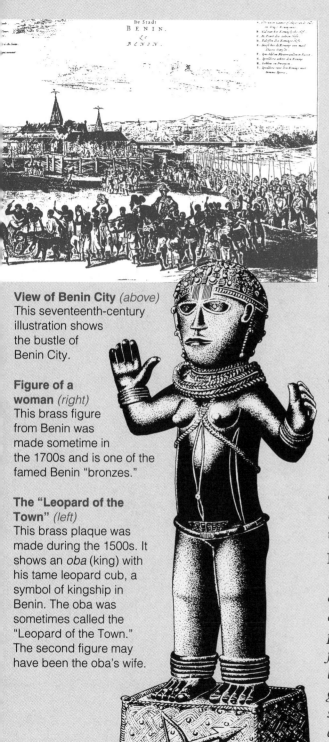

View of Benin City *(above)*
This seventeenth-century illustration shows the bustle of Benin City.

Figure of a woman *(right)*
This brass figure from Benin was made sometime in the 1700s and is one of the famed Benin "bronzes."

The "Leopard of the Town" *(left)*
This brass plaque was made during the 1500s. It shows an *oba* (king) with his tame leopard cub, a symbol of kingship in Benin. The oba was sometimes called the "Leopard of the Town." The second figure may have been the oba's wife.

Ivory sistrum *(right)*
This elaborately carved ivory artifact is from the sixteenth century. It is a *sistrum*, a rattlelike musical instrument with bells inside.

The old city

A Flemish writer describing the city in the 1600s said it was large and prosperous. It was about 5 or 6 miles (8–9 km) around, protected by a high wall — except where it was defended by marshes or impenetrable vegetation. The streets were broad and the royal headquarters contained a number of magnificent buildings. The British took over the Kingdom of Benin in 1897 and made it part of the protectorate *(colony) of Southern Nigeria. In the same year, British forces stormed Benin City and burned part of it as punishment for the massacre of an unarmed trade mission. Many brass, copper, and ivory works of art were seized and sent to London. The descendants of the Bini still flourish in and around Benin City. The language is spoken by more than two million people in southwestern Nigeria, who are now mostly known as the Edo.*

Religious beliefs

The people of Benin had many gods, some regarded as beneficial and some not. Osanobua, the creator, and his son Olokun were gods who brought prosperity and long life. Ogun was the god of farmers, hunters, and metalworkers. Ohgiuwu, the bringer of death, and Esu, the trickster, were other gods. The Bini believed that every human had a spirit of destiny, called an Ehi, which the soul created before birth in conversation with Osanobua.

    The religion of old Benin is very similar to that practiced by the present-day Yoruba people.

Appendix: West African languages

Africans often identify themselves by the language they speak, rather than, or in addition to, their ethnic origin or nationality. Language classification in Africa is complex, however; more than 1,000 languages are spoken, most of them "home" languages (native to the continent) and the rest introduced by groups from Europe and Asia who settled in or colonized regions of Africa. Also, many Muslims learn Arabic because it is the language of the *Koran,* Islam's sacred text. Hausa and

Dyula are widely used as common languages, and various Creole languages, such as Liberian Krio, are spoken. Creole languages combine elements of African and European languages. As a result of this diversity, many West Africans can speak more than one language.

Among the languages introduced to Africa are English, French, Spanish, Portuguese, Afrikaans, Urdu, Hindi, Gujarati, and Malagasy. English, French, and Portuguese are commonly spoken in many West African countries as they

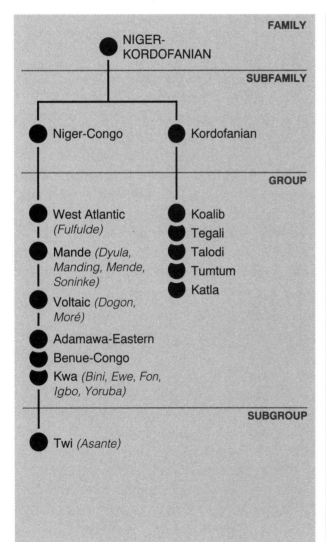

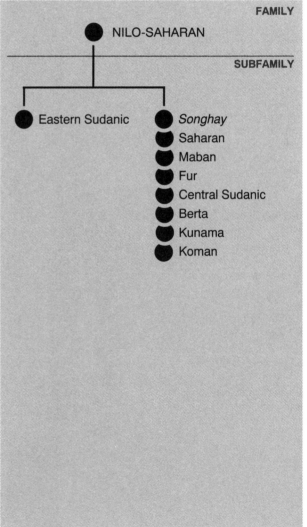

were the languages of the main colonial powers and are still used today as common languages.

The home languages of Africa are divided into four language **families**: Niger-Kordofanian, Nilo-Saharan, Afroasiatic, and Khoisan. Within these families are several **subfamilies**, many of which are also divided into **groups** and **subgroups** – only the relevant subgroups are shown. For example, Asante – the language of the Asante people – is a dialect of Twi, which belongs to the Kwa language group of the Niger-Congo subfamily, which is part of the Niger-Kordofanian language family. Some groups are themselves languages, as in the case of Songhay; other groups constitute clusters of individual languages, such as the Mande group.

Within the diagram below, the languages of the peoples profiled in this volume are printed in *italics*. This appendix can be therefore be used to identify the subgroup, group, subfamily, and family of each language and to see how the different languages relate to one another.

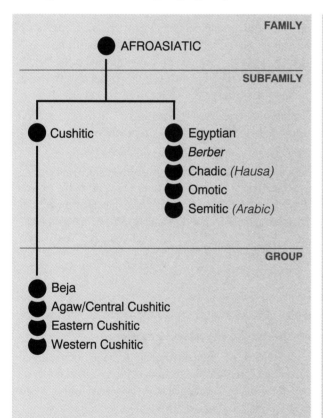

FAMILY
● AFROASIATIC

SUBFAMILY
● Cushitic
● Egyptian
● *Berber*
● Chadic *(Hausa)*
● Omotic
● Semitic *(Arabic)*

GROUP
● Beja
● Agaw/Central Cushitic
● Eastern Cushitic
● Western Cushitic

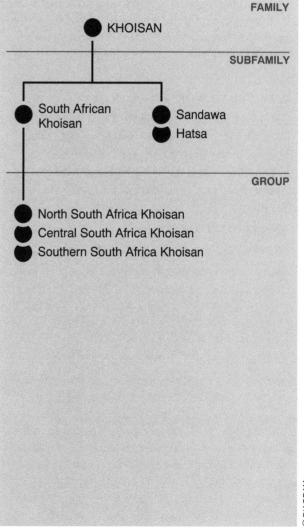

FAMILY
● KHOISAN

SUBFAMILY
● South African Khoisan
● Sandawa
● Hatsa

GROUP
● North South Africa Khoisan
● Central South Africa Khoisan
● Southern South Africa Khoisan

Glossary

Bold words are cross-references to other glossary entries.

African Franc Zone A group of African countries whose currencies are linked with the French franc at a fixed exchange rate. The currency that these countries use is called the **CFA** or **CFA franc**. The African Franc Zone countries of West Africa are Senegal, Mali, Ivory Coast, Burkina Faso, Niger, Chad, Cameroon, Togo, and Benin. The remainder of the African Franc Zone countries are in Central Africa.

Afro-Beat A form of popular West African music.

akple A mixture of corn and cassava flour used to make a food that is usually eaten with meat or vegetable stew.

Ala In the Igbo religion, Ala is generally considered to be the Earth goddess. Shrines are dedicated to Ala, and the Igbo's most important festival, the Yam Festival, is celebrated in her honor.

Allah The Muslim name for God.

Amma The Dogon supreme god.

Anansi A spider character, known as a trickster, who features in many West African folktales. Anansi also appears in Caribbean storytelling as African folklore was taken to the Americas by slaves taken from Africa.

appliqué A decoration or trimming of one material sewn or fixed onto another.

asantehene The Asante king.

awoamefia The **dukowo** head of the Anlo Ewe.

balafon A percussion musical instrument, similar to the xylophone, widely used throughout Africa – in West Africa by the Mossi, among others. It is usually made of wooden keys that may be attached to calabashes of different sizes or a wooden frame.

bolombatos Manding gourd harps.

bridewealth A practice common among African people in which a marriage between a couple is sealed with a gift – often cattle, but it may be cash or other animals – from the groom to the bride's family. The bride is not regarded as property; the payment is usually considered to be compensation to the bride's family for loss of a working member, or it may be a token payment as a mark of respect. Part of the bridewealth may be used by the couple to set up home together.

calabash A type of gourd whose hollowed-out shell has a wide variety of uses from container to musical instrument. Calabashes often figure in African legends and mythology where the two halves are used, for example, to symbolize the union of Heaven and Earth, man and woman, or land and sky.

caliph Arabic for "successor": an Islamic ruler.

canopy A layer in a forest formed by the crowns (branches and leaves) of trees. **Rainforests** have more than one canopy. The upper canopy occurs at a height of 90 to 150 ft (30–45 m), but this layer is pierced by occasional tall trees called **emergents**. One or two lower canopies occur at roughly 60 ft (20 m) and 30 ft (10 m). The canopies are inhabited by tree-dwelling species such as birds, bats, and monkeys. The sunlight is strong and the vegetation is thick and virtually impenetrable. Below the canopies, relatively little sunlight penetrates down to ground level where the vegetation is sparser.

Casamance-style music A percussive style from a region of the same name in Senegal and Gambia.

CFA An abbreviation for "Communauté Financière Africaine," CFA is the currency used by the West and Central African countries that form the **African Franc Zone**. The CFA franc is on a fixed exchange rate with the French franc. The initials originally stood for "Colonies Français d'Afrique," but were changed after West Africa became independent from colonial rule.

CFA franc *see* **CFA**

Chukwu A supreme being acknowledged by some Igbo groups. Chukwu is the creator of the visible universe.

circumcise To carry out **circumcision**.

circumcision For men, this involves the removal of all or part of the foreskin. Some cultures practice female circumcision, which ranges in severity from minor to major genital mutilation. This is highly controversial, however, and is opposed by many African women.

clan A group of people, usually several **lineages**, related by ancestry or marriage. Clan members often often claim descent from a common ancestor or ancestors.

compound An enclosure containing living quarters. Compound is often used to refer to a group of buildings lived in by members of the same family.

copra The dried "meat" of the coconut. Copra is the source of coconut oil.

couscous A spicy dish originating in North Africa that consists of a steamed, coarse-ground grain such as semolina. Couscous is popular in the semidesert Sahel region of West Africa.

deforestation The clearing of trees in a forest. In the African **rainforests**, huge tracts of land are being cleared of trees every year. The reasons are primarily economic. In poorer countries, where most rainforests are, their clearance is a way of raising much-needed cash to pay off debts to foreign banks and governments. Also, the growth of urban areas has led to the intensification and extensification of agriculture: more land is needed to farm and this land is farmed more intensively, leaving it little time to recover. In forest areas, this can result in a permanent loss of forest if the land is not allowed time to recover from cultivation. Deforestation causes soil deterioration, which can lead to soil erosion. It can also indirectly lead to a decrease in rainfall as trees are an essential part of the climatic processes that produce rain.

delta An apron of land made from sediment deposited at the mouth of a river where the main stream splits up into several distributaries.

desertification A process of land degradation in which previously fertile land can be turned into barren land or desert. It is usually caused by **drought** or the overuse of fragile lands. Desertification only occurs in drylands, which have low, infrequent, and irregular rainfall and high temperatures. This includes the Sahel semidesert region in West Africa, where desertification has become an increasingly urgent problem in recent decades.

divination A common feature of many African religions, divination is practiced by **diviners** who use various tools (such as wooden figures, plants, bones, or seeds) to divine the spiritual cause of a specific problem such as illness, accident, or misfortune.

diviner A religious practitioner who practices **divination**.

drought Water shortage caused by a prolonged period of inadequate rainfall. Drought can have a devastating affect on the land and people who make their living from the land. Drought in the Sahel region of West Africa in recent decades has led to large numbers of refugees and dramatically reduced the number of people following **nomadic** ways of life.

dufia The head of a village in Ewe society.

dukowo A council of Ewe **dufias** who would advise the overall leader of a whole region. In the past, the Ewe were divided into ten such **dukowo**.

dyamu Malinke word for a group of people who share the same name, male ancestors, and **taboos**.

dyeli A name for professional singers (bards) among the Bambara and Malinke. Dyeli are often involved in maintaining oral history as their songs retell and preserve Manding history.

Ehi The people of the historic Kingdom of Benin believed that every human had a spirit of destiny, called a Ehi, which the soul created before birth in conversation with **Osanobua**.

emergents Occasional tall trees that rise above the upper **canopy** of a tropical **rainforest**. The upper canopy occurs at a height of 90 to 150 ft (30–45 m), but emergents can reach a height of over 190 ft (60 m).

emir The ruler, prince, or commander of an Islamic state.

epiphytes Plants that grow on other plants but are not parasites. Many epiphytes, or air plants, grow on the branches of trees in **rainforests**.

Esu A god of the historic Kingdom of Benin and of the Yoruba people. Often described as the "trickster god," Esu (or Eshu) tells **Olodumare** of the activities of other **orisa** and of people.

Ethiopian faunal realm A biogeographical zone that includes most of sub-Saharan Africa. Animals of this realm include lions, elephants, and giraffes.

fama A Bambara local leader.

gandu The basic unit of the cooperative system in which most Hausa agricultural work is carried out.

geerewol A dance performed at a Fulani **worso**. These dances prove the ability of men to attract women.

Gelede Festivals incorporating masked dancers held by the Yoruba at regular intervals. Now largely to entertain, they were once intended to appease local witches.

ghana The title – meaning war-chief – of the kings of the ancient empire of Wagadu. It later came to be used as the name for the medieval Empire of Ghana.

ginna The "great house," generally lived in by the male head of a Dogon village or **lineage**.

granary A building or room in which grain is stored.

griot A general West African name for storytellers, singers, and musicians.

groundnut A group of plants including the peanut, which is a major cash crop and food item in many West African countries.

hakpa A session at a Ewe festival that is a general singing practice for everybody.

hale Societies to which many Mende belong. Among the most important hale are **Poro** and **Sande**. Others include **Humui**, **Njayei**, **Yassi**, and **Kpa**. Until recently the working of these socieites was kept from noninitiates, so they are often refered to as "secret" societies.

halo A feature of some Ewe festivals, it is an exchange of insulting songs between neighboring villages.

harmattan A cool, dry, dusty wind from the Sahara Desert that blows toward the West African coast, especially from November through March.

havalu A session at a Ewe festival in which the composer teaches a new song to his fellow drummers.

highlife A dance music that is often considered the national music of Ghana. Early forms of it originated in Ghana's southern Cape Coast area in the 1880s. The name "highlife" was coined during the 1920s in the context of high-class Ghanaian ballroom dance orchestras. Highlife incorporates African guitar techniques brought from Liberia by Creole mariners in the beginning of the twentieth century, and has also been influenced by colonial military bands. It became very popular during and after World War II but declined in the 1980s. More recently, Ghanaian musicians have been using computer aids to produce disco-orientated forms.

hogon The spiritual leader of the Dogon, responsible for, among other things, preserving myths.

Humui A Mende **hale** that helps to regulate sexual behaviour. The rules of Humui prohibit certain kinds of sexual relationships, such as those with girls under the age of puberty or with nursing mothers.

Ifijoku A god worshipped by the Igbo as the giver and protector of yams – a form of sweet potato that plays a central part in the village economy.

imraguen A Moorish social class of largely itinerant fisherman who live along the coast of Mauritania.

indigo A deep blue dye usually made from certain plants.

inselbergs Isolated rocky hills rising abruptly from a flat plain or plateau.

invertebrates Any animal without a backbone.

jali Manding term for **griot**; the traditional caste of musician storytellers.

jihad An Islamic holy war against nonbelievers undertaken by Muslims. (In the 1670s, the Fulani began a series of jihads against their non-Muslim neighbors, which lasted for almost the next two centuries. During this period Futa Toro, Futa Djallon, Wuli, and Bundu were established as jihadist states.)

juju Yoruba urban music of Nigeria.

kafu A group of Malinke villages making up a distinct social unit, headed by a **mansa**.

kalunga A type of **talking drum** from Nigeria.

Kanaga The "Hand of God," the name of a Dogon mask worn by newly initiated young men.

kente Colorful cloth generally made by Asante weavers and considered the national dress of Ghana. Kente cloth is distinctive for its complex patterns.

keta Strip-woven cloth generally made by Ewe weavers that uses contrasting **warp** and **weft** colors with inlaid designs. It is similar to Asante **kente** cloth.

kize-uzi Fonio grain, the smallest cultivated seed. The Dogon call it "the little thing."

kontingo A three-stringed, Manding musical instrument.

kora A popular stringed musical instrument played widely throughout West Africa but thought to originate from Manding culture.

Koran The sacred book of the Islamic religion, believed by Muslims to be the word of **Allah**.

Kpa A Mende **hale**. Kpa members, who are largely men, are trained to use herbs to treat minor ailments such as toothache or earache.

kpegisu One of the oldest traditional Ewe drums, kpegisu was probably originally a war drum.

kpezi A clay and raffia drum used at Fon funerals.

lineage An extended family that shares a common ancestor. If this ancestor is male and descent is traced from father to son, then the lineage is patrilineal. If the ancestor is female and descent is traced from mother to daughter, then the lineage is matrilineal. Groups of several related lineages are often organized into **clans**.

Lisa The Sun god of the Fon religion who represents strength and endurance and who causes day and heat. He is the son of **Mawa**.

lost-beetle *see* **lost-wax**

lost-wax A metal-casting method used by Asante goldsmiths and other metalworkers for centuries. A wax model of the object is made and encased in a clay mold. When the clay mold is heated, the wax melts and molten metal is poured into its place through a hole in the mold. The lost-beetle method, which may be even older, is similar but uses a real object such as a beetle or seed rather than a wax model.

mangrove forests A forest of mangrove trees – tropical evergreen trees with intertwining roots that form a dense thicket. Mangrove forests generally occur along coasts and rivers, where their networks of roots help to anchor the silty soil. This can create areas of swampy land, hence their alternative name of mangrove swamps. Many West African mangrove forests have been cleared for rice cultivation. This **deforestation** is a threat to the great variety of animal and marine life that inhabits these areas.

mangrove swamps *see* **mangrove forests**

mansa A Malinke chief or king.

marabout A Muslim holy man or hermit, especially among the Moors of Mauritania and the Berbers of North and West Africa.

masquerade A festival at which masks and costumes are worn. Many African cultures have rich heritages that include masquerades, which when taken to the Americas by slaves became the ancestors of many modern carnivals.

Mawa The creator god of the Fon religion. Mawa is the Moon god and has both male and female characteristics. Mawa is also associated with **Mawu**, the supreme god of the Ewe religion, which is related to the Fon religion.

mawe The basic Mende social and economic unit.

Mawu The supreme god of the Ewe religion. Mawu is usually only approached through the **trowo**. Mawu is associated with **Mawa**, the creator god of the Fon religion, which is closely related to the Ewe religion.

minsereh Carved wooden female figures used by the Mende **Yassi** society for healing and **divination**.

mogho naba The supreme ruler, or king, of the Mossi.

monoculture The continuous growing of one particular type of crop.

montane forests "Montane" literally means from, or inhabiting, mountainous regions. A montane forest is made up of trees and vegetation that prefer the cool and moist conditions of highland areas.

mosque Muslim house of worship.

mud cloths Bambara mud cloths are woven by men but bear geometric designs applied by women. A pattern is painted onto a just-dyed cloth using mud, then soap, then more mud. When the cloth is dry, the mud is scraped off, which removes the dye from the area beneath and leaves the pattern exposed. Usually, mud cloths are made with a pale pattern on a dark background.

naba Chiefs in Mossi society.

nakomsé Literally meaning "the right and power to rule," the nakomsé is the Mossi ruling class, and was made up of chiefs, kings, and emperors in the past.

Ngewo The supreme god of the Mende religion.

ngoni A four-stringed lute, in the past played by Bambara musicians to inspire men to fight.

Njayei A Mende **hale**. Njayei initiates use herbs and other substances to cure mental illness, which is attributed to breaching this society's rules.

nomad Used to describe many, usually desert-living, peoples who follow a particular lifestyle. Nomads are "wanderers" (the word derives from "nomas," Latin for "wandering shepherd"), but their movements are dictated by trade or the needs of their herds for pasture and water.

nomadic Characteristic of, or like, **nomads** and their ways of life.

nomadism Used to describe the lifestyle of a **nomad**.

nomori A type of figurine made by Mende artisans.

ntomos Societies among the Bambara and Malinke whose responsibility it is to prepare young boys for **circumcision** and initiation into adulthood.

nyamakala Professional groups representing different craftworkers among the Bambara and Malinke.

Nyame The supreme god of the Asante religion.

nyonyosé A Mossi social class comprising the ordinary civilians. Nyonyosé literally means "ancient ones" or "children of the earth."

oasis A fertile pocket in the desert where the underground water reaches the surface.

oba A position held by a descendant of a town's founder in Yoruba society, passing in turn to princes from several ruling houses. Also, the title of the king of the historic Kingdom of Benin.

Obatala The most important of the Yoruba **orisa**, Obatala is the chief representative of **Olodumare** on Earth. Obatala was taught to create the human form into which Olodumare then put life.

oding A traditional flute from Cameroon usually played only by women. The oding is filled with water.

Ogun A god of the historic Kingdom of Benin, Ogun was the god of farmers, hunters, and metalworkers. In the Yoruba religion, Ogun is the god associated with iron and is often shown respect by taxi drivers who have singled him out for protection while they drive their vehicles.

ohemmaa Commonly refered to as the "**queen mother**" in some literature, the ohemmaa is actually the most senior Asante woman and not neccessarily the mother of the **asantehene**.

Ohiguwu A god of the historic Kingdom of Benin, Ohiguwu is the bringer of death.

Olodumare The supreme god (the owner of Heaven) in the Yoruba religion.

Olukon A god of the historic Kingdom of Benin, son of **Osanbua**, who brought prosperity and long life.

onigi Meaning "sticks" in Yoruba, onigi refers to hairstyles in which the hair is wrapped to resemble sticks.

orisa Yoruba spirits or deities, each with its own cult, priests, temples, and shrines. There are more than four hundred orisa (or orisha) in the Yoruba religion.

Osanobua The creator-god of the historic Kingdom of Benin, Osanobua brought prosperity and long life.

pastoral *see* **pastoralist**

pastoralism Used to describe the lifestyle of a **pastoralist**.

pastoralist A person who raises livestock.

Poro A Mende **hale** for men. Initiates are taken to a camp in the forest where they live in seclusion for weeks. Poro teaches Mende ideals of manhood, settles local disputes, and regulates market trading.

protectorate A state or territory that is controlled by a usually stronger nation. In particular it is used to refer to the colonies established by Europeans in Africa. African rulers were often misled, forced, or tricked into signing protectorate treaties on the understanding that they were only a promise by the Europeans to protect their country from agression, and were not told that the agreement gave away sovereignty over their land.

queen mother A position of prestige conferred on the most senior woman in Fon and Asante society. Also, used in the past in the historic Kingdom of Benin.

rainforest Dense forest found in tropical areas with heavy rainfall. The trees are nearly all broadleaved evergreens, such as ironwood and mahogany. The crowns of these trees merge to form several canopies of leaves and branches. The upper **canopy** is pierced by even taller trees called **emergents**. The temperature is about 27 °C (80 °F) throughout the year with eighty-percent humidity. Up to fifty percent of the rain that falls on a rainforest consists of water released into the atmosphere by the forest itself, so without the forest, the rainfall in the region would be greatly reduced. Also, rainforests are ecologically very rich and house a greater variety of flora and fauna than most other environments. **Deforestation** is the biggest threat to the rainforests and great stretches are cut down every year for fuelwood, to clear land for farming, or to provide timber to export.

rias Long narrow inlets of the seacoast that were formerly valleys which have been submerged by a rise in the sea level.

Sande A Mende **hale** for women. Initiates are taken to a camp in the forest where they live in seclusion for weeks. Sande mostly teaches Mende ideals of womanhood though it also provides healthcare and advice for women.

Sango The Yoruba **orisa** associated with thunderstorms and the anger of **Olodumare**. Sango (or Shango) artefacts are usually recognizable for the inclusion of a double ax-head motif.

savanna Open grasslands, often with scattered bushes or trees, characteristic of tropical Africa.

seminomadic pastoralism A form of **pastoralism** involving the seasonal movement of livestock.

Sharia Islamic holy law.

shifting cultivation A land use system in which a patch of land is cleared and cultivated until its fertility diminishes, and then abandoned until restored naturally. This type of farming has long been practiced in Africa.

sistrum A rattlelike musical instrument with bells.

slash and burn A method of cultivation in which the forest is cleared by cutting down and burning the trees and other vegetation for temporary agricultural use. Although labor intensive, this method is ideally suited to the tropics. It allows the soil to recuperate, and the burning of vegetation fixes nutrients in the soil.

Sowo The spirit of **Sande**.

Sowo-wui Wooden heads that are part of **Sowo** costumes of the **Sande** society of the Mende people.

subsistence agriculture A type of farming in which all or most of the crop is consumed by the farmer and his family, leaving little or nothing to be marketed.

taboo A social prohibition or restriction laid down by culture, tradition, or convention that forbids, for example, certain actions and helps to define acceptable behavior.

talking drums Drums that can be used to mimic the tonal qualities of African languages. Talking drums probably originate from Wolof culture.

Tisiefa In the Ewe religion, Tisiefa means the "Other World," which is where people go after death.

togu na An open-sided building in the main square of a Dogon village. It is used for council meetings.

tro A spirit or deity in the Ewe religion. The plural is trowo. Trowo are similar to the Fon **vodun**.

trowo *see* **tro**

Tyi-wara A mythical half-man, half-antelope attributed with the introduction of cultivation to the Bambara.

underemployment A situation in which although few people are totally unemployed many do not have enough work to provide for their needs. For example, this can mean that people may have a few part-time, low-paid jobs that do not fully exploit their potential. In Africa, few people can afford to be unemployed as there are rarely social security systems on which they can rely. A lack of job opportunities, however, means that people are forced to take or create whatever work is available.

urbanization The process of making a predominately rural area more industrialized and urban.

vodoun *see* vodu

vodu A spirit or deity of the Fon religion. The plural of vodu is vodun (or vodoun, which is also an alternative name for the Fon religion). Vodun are very similar to the **trowo** of the Ewe religion. "Vodu" is probably the origin of the word "voodoo," a term that embodies Western misunderstandings about the Fon religion – "voodoo" is often incorrectly described as involving "black magic," witchcraft, and the worship of fetishes (idols).

vodun *see* **vodu**

warp Lengthwise threads in a woven cloth.

wattle-and-daub A building technique using a woven latticework of sticks thickly plastered with mud or clay.

weft Threads that go across the **warp** in a woven cloth.

worso A Wodaabe (Fulani) annual festival that celebrates marriages and births of the previous year.

yaake A dance performed at a **worso** in which men are judged for charm, magnetism, and personality by elders.

Yassi A Mende **hale** that is devoted to the art of spiritual healing. Female Yassi **diviners** use **minsereh** figures.

Yemoja A female **orisa**, associated with water, rivers, lakes, and streams.

zilin A Fon singing technique similar to the blues.

Index

Peoples pages and special features are in **bold**; *italic* page numbers refer to illustrations, captions, or maps.

Index